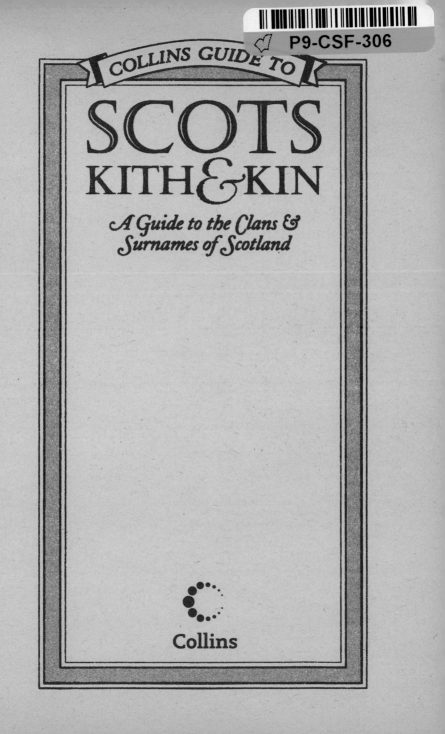

COLLINS GUIDE TO

SCOTS
KITH&KIN

*A Guide to the Clans &
Surnames of Scotland*

Collins

HarperCollins Publishers
77-85 Fulham Palace Road
London W6 8JB

www.collins.co.uk

Collins is a registered trademark of
HarperCollins Publishers Ltd.

12 11 10 09 08

10 9 8 7 6 5 4 3 2 1

First published in 1953
Revised edition published 1989
This edition published 2008

A catalogue record for this book is available
from the British Library.

ISBN-13 978-0-00-727328-7
ISBN-10 0-00-727328-2

Collins uses papers that are natural, renewable and
recyclable products made from wood grown in
sustainable forests. The manufacturing processes
conform to the environmental regulations of the
country of origin.

Printed in Great Britain by Clays Ltd, St Ives plc

Mixed Sources
Product group from well-managed
forests and other controlled sources
www.fsc.org Cert no. SW-COC-1806
© 1996 Forest Stewardship Council
FSC

CONTENTS

INTRODUCTION

An old Gaelic proverb says, 'Remember the men from whence you came.' By 'men', of course, it means humankind, embracing women, which in fact sums up how unfair — and distorting — is the basic principle of surnames. By law, throughout Britain, we are required to take the surname of our father and his father before him, not that of our mother or even her father's family. The word 'surname' refers to another name which has been 'added on' to a first or Christian name. Just how, and when, your family name was added to a forbear's first name can vary enormously. In Lowland Scotland some territorial names were being introduced as surnames in the 11th century, mostly by landed people. Then we see centuries of surname proliferation as men became known by their trades ('Taillour', 'Porter'), proximity to geographical features ('Wood', 'Burnbank'), personal characteristics or colouring ('Little', 'Reid'), or by connection to their father's name ('Johnson', 'Donaldson').

This last style, called patronymics, was popular when surnames came widely into use in the Highlands in the 16th century. Gradually (and not until this century in the Northern Isles), the patronymic system was replaced by the adoption of a fixed family name taken from an ancestral figure, or 'namefather', like Gregor, brother of King Kenneth MacAlpine in the 9th century, from whom the MacGregors take their name. This removed the practice of members of a generation taking their surnames from their own fathers' Christian names. John Robertson's father was *Robert* Williamson whose father was *William* Thomson whose father was *Thomas* Davidson whose father was David. . . . The process becomes confusing when you find that your MacDonald forbear was the son of a Donald Campbell.

In the great ancestry game, you will learn quickly that your surname is only the tip of the genetic iceberg. If your genuinely MacDonald forbear had found himself isolated in the heart of Campbell country ten generations ago, had married Jean Campbell and seen his sons and grandsons married to Campbell girls, you could find yourself today with a bank of forbears totalling 1,022, all of whom were Campbells except yourself and the nine named MacDonald in the direct male line. But the even more awesome thought is that if just *one* of those 1,022 forbears (your parents, four grandparents, eight great-grandparents, etc) had died in childhood, you would not be here today. So you are much, much more than just your surname.

This book is a key to understanding all the other names which you are heir to. A simple, easy-to-use key if you remember the following rules:

★ The sound of a name is generally more important than its spelling, which would have been standardised only comparatively recently. Shakespeare, who was somewhat literate, spelt his own surname in over twenty different ways in his lifetime.

★ Including spelling variations, there are over 16,000 Scottish surnames, but fewer than 3,000 of these are of Highland origin and associated with clans. The majority of Scots throughout history lived in the Lowlands and developed a culture which produced the majority of Scotland's genius but without the glamour which is now associated with their Highland cousins.

★ *Mac* is part of many Scottish surnames and simply means 'son'. It is popularly believed that names beginning with *Mc* are of Irish origin and those with *Mac*, Scottish. This is not the case. *Mac* is the standardised prefix used today, but a hundred years ago it was commonly abbreviated in written records to *Mc* or even *M'*.

★ The association of certain common names with a clan, e.g. Reid, Smith, is generally because there were prominent families of that name connected with that clan and not that it had the monopoly of ruddy-faced or red-haired people or of clansmen with metal-working skills.

Micheil MacDonald, FSA Scot.
Director, Highland Tryst Museum
Crieff

WHAT IS YOUR CLAN OR DISTRICT CONNECTION?

Scottish surnames alphabetically arranged to show clan or sept connection, or approximate district or century earliest known in Scotland.

Cross-references to other names in this list are printed in capitals. The names of associated clans (whose histories are given in *Clans of Scotland* starting on page 53) are printed in italic type.

SURNAME	CLAN OR DISTRICT SOURCE	KEY TO MAP
ABBOT, ABBOTT	Fife etc. 14th c.; *MACNAB*	F6
ABBOTSON	*MACNAB*	F6
ABERCROMBIE	Fife (place, now St Monans) 15th c.	
ABERNETHY	Strathearn 12th c.; *FRASER*; *LESLIE*	K3, J4
ADAIR	Galloway 14th c.; from EDGAR	
ADAM, ADAMS	Fife etc. 13th c.; *GORDON*	J4
ADAMSON	Berwickshire 13th c., Aberdeen 14th c.; *GORDON*; *MACKINTOSH*	J4, G4
ADDIE, ADIE	Fife 13th c.; *GORDON*	J4
ADDISON	Peeblesshire etc. 14th c.; *GORDON*	J4
AFFLECK	From AUCHINLECK, Angus 14th c.	
AGNEW	Galloway 11th c.	E9
AIKMAN	Lanarkshire 13th c.	
AINSLIE	Roxburghshire etc. 13th c.	
AIRD	Ayrshire 16th c.	
AIRLIE	*OGILVIE*	J5
AIRTH	Stirlingshire 12th c.; *GRAHAM*	G6
AITCHISON	E. Lothian 14th c.; *GORDON*	J4
AITKEN, AIKEN	Aberdeen 15th c.; *GORDON*	J4
AITKENHEAD	Lanarkshire (place) 13th c.	
ALASTAIR	Same as ALEXANDER	
ALCOCK	From ALLAN	
ALEXANDER	*MACALISTER*; *MACDONALD*	D7
	MACDONNELL of Glengarry	E4
ALISON, ALLISON	From MACALISTER: also ALLANSON	
ALLAN, ALLEN	Same as MACALLAN	
ALLANACH	Aberdeenshire, see MACALLAN	
ALLANSON	From MACALLAN	
ALLARDYCE	Mearns (place) 13th c.; *GRAHAM*	G6
ALLISTER	Same as ALEXANDER	
ALPIN, ALPINE	Clan ALPIN	E6
ALVES	Moray (Alves) 13th c.	
AMBROSE	Glasgow 15th c., Edinburgh etc. 17th c.	
ANDERSON	Peebles etc. 13th c. *ROSS*	G3
	Islay, *MACDONALD*	D7
ANDISON	From ANDERSON	
ANDREW, ANDREWS	Dumfries, Aberdeen 14th c.; *ROSS*	G3
ANGUS	Angus county 13th c.; *MACINNES*	D5
ANNAL, ANNALL	Fife 16th c.	
ANNAN, ANNAND	Annandale, also Angus 13th c.	
ANSTRUTHER	Fife (place) 13th c.	

SURNAME	CLAN OR DISTRICT SOURCE	KEY TO MAP
ANTHONY	Roxburghshire 13th c.	
ARBUCKLE	Lanarkshire (place) 15th c.	
ARBUTHNOT	Kincardineshire (place) 12th c.	J5
ARCHER	Ayrshire 13th c., Angus 15th c.	
ARCHIBALD	Roxburghshire 14th c.; also GILLESPIE	
ARGYL	*MACGREGOR*	F6
ARMOUR	'Armourer': Peebles, Angus etc. 14th c.	
ARMSTRONG	Clan *ARMSTRONG*	J6
ARNOLD, ARNOULD	Selkirkshire, W. Lothian, 13th c.	
ARNOT, ARNOTT	Kinross-shire 12th c., Ayrshire 15th c.	
ARROL	Perthshire (Errol) 16th c.; *HAY*	I6
ARROWSMITH	*MACGREGOR*	F6
ARTHUR, ARTHURSON	*MACARTHUR*	F6
ASKEY	*MACLEOD* of Lewis	C4
ATKIN, ATKINS	Same as AITKEN	
ATKINSON	Same as AITCHISON	
AUCHINCLOSS	Ayrshire (Kilmarnock) 15th c.	
AUCHINLECK	Ayrshire (Cumnock) 13th c.	
AUCHTERLONIE	Angus (place near Forfar) 13th c.	
AULAY	*MACAULAY*; *MACLEOD* of Lewis	F7, B2
AULD	Ayrshire and Perth 13th c.	
AUSTIN	*KEITH*	K5
AYSON	*MACINTOSH* of Glentilt	H5
AYTON, AYTOUN	Berwickshire (place) 12th c.; *HOME*	K7
BADENOCH	Badenoch to Aberdeenshire 15th c.	
BAIKIE	Orkney 16th c.	
BAILEY, BAILLIE	Lothian 14th c., Lamington 16th c.	
BAIN	Perth 14th c.; *MACKAY*	F2
BAINES	Fife (St Andrews) 16th c.	
BAIRD	Lanarkshire 13th c.	H7
BAIRNSFATHER	East Lothian 16th c.	
BAIRNSON	Caithness 16th c.; *MATHESON*	E4
BALCANQUALL	Fife (Strathmiglo) 14th c.	
BALD	Peeblesshire and Perth 13th c.	
BALDERSTON	W. Lothian (place) 13th c.	
BALFOUR	Fife (Markinch) 14th c.	
BALLANTYNE	Hawick 15th c.; and from BANNATYNE	
BALLINGALL	Kinross-shire (place) 15th c.	
BALLOCH, BALLACH	Lennox 15th c., *MACDONALD*	D7
BALMAIN	Kincardineshire (place) 16th c.	
BALNEAVES	Angus 14th c.; *MURRAY*	G5
BALSILLIE	Fife (Leslie) 16th c.	
BANKS	Berwick 13th c.; Orkney 17th c.	
BANNATYNE	*CAMPBELL*; *STUART* of Bute	E6, E7
BANNERMAN	Aberdeen 14th c.; *FORBES*	J4
BAPTIE	Berwickshire 13th c.	
BARBER, BARBOUR	Ayrshire 13th c.	
BARCLAY	Aberdeenshire etc. 12th c.	J4, J5
BARD, BARDE	Same as BAIRD	
BARKER	Stirlingshire and Lothians 13th c.	
BARLAS	Perthshire 17th c.	
BARNES, BARNS	Aberdeenshire 15th c.	
BARNETSON	Caithness 16th c.	
BARON, BARRON	Angus 15th c.; Inverness, *ROSE*	H3
BARR	Ayrshire 14th c.	

SURNAME	CLAN OR DISTRICT SOURCE	KEY TO MAP
BARRACK	Aberdeenshire (Meldrum) 16th c.	
BARRIE, BARRY	Angus 14th c.; *FARQUHARSON*;	
	GORDON	I5, J4
BARROWDALE	*MACGREGOR*	F6
BARTHOLOMEW	Midlothian 13th c.; *MACFARLANE*	F6
BARTIE, BARTY,	From BARTHOLOMEW	
BARTLEMAN,		
BARTLET, BARLETT		
BARTON	Ayrshire, Berwickshire 13th c.	
BATCHELOR	E. Lothian 13th c., Angus 15th c.	
BATHGATE	W. Lothian 13th c.	
BAUCHOPE, BACHOP	From WAUCHOPE	
BAXTER	Lothian 12th c.; *MACMILLAN*	D7
BAYNE, BAYNES	See BAIN and BAINES	
BEAN	*MACBEAN*	I4
BEATH	*MACDONALD*; *MACLEAN*	C3, D7; B5, D6
BEATON	*MACLEAN*, and from BETHUNE	D6, I6
BEATSON	Dumfriesshire 14th c., Fife 17th c.	
BEATTIE, BEATTY	Dumfriesshire etc. 14th c.; *MACBETH*	I3
BEAUMONT	E. Fife 13th c.	
BECK	Dumfriesshire 14th c.	
BEE	Angus 16th c., Edinburgh etc. 17th c.	
BEGBIE	Haddington 16th c.	
BEGG	Lennox 13th c.; *DRUMMOND*	H6
BEGLAND	*MACGREGOR*	F6
BELFORD	Berwick 12th c., Stirling 14th c.	
BELFRAGE	W. Fife, Kinross from BEVERIDGE	
BELL	Dunkeld, Dumfries 13th c; *MACMILLAN*	D7
BELTON	E. Lothian 13th c.; *MACBETH*	I3
BENHAM	Kincardineshire (Benholm) 13th c.	
BENNET, BENNETT	Roxburghshire 16th c., Fife 17th c.	
BENNIE, BENNY	Gowrie 13th c., Aberdeen 14th c.	
BENVIE	Dundee 13th c.	
BENZIE, BENZIES	Aberdeenshire (Inverurie) 15th c.	
BERNARD	Perthshire 13th c.	
BERRIE, BERRY	Fife, Angus 14th c.; *FORBES*	J4
BERTRAM	W. Fife 13th c., Edinburgh 15th c.	
BERWICK	Berwick, to Roxburgh etc. 13th c.	
BEST	Edinburgh 15th c., Aberdeen 17th c.	
BETHUNE	Angus 12th c., Fife 13th c.; *MACBETH*	I6, I3
	MACDONALD; *MACLEOD*	D7, C4
BETT	Edinburgh 14th c., Fife, Angus 15th c.	
BEVERIDGE	Fife 14th c.	
BEWS, BEWES	Orkney 17th c.	
BEY	From MACBEY; *MACLEAN*	B5, D6
BIE	Same as BEE	
BIGAM, BIGGAM	Edinburgh 15th c.	
BIGGAR	Lanarkshire 12th c.	
BILSLAND	Ayrshire 16th c.	
BINNIE	*MACBEAN*	I4
BINNIE, BINNING	W. Lothian 13th c.	
BIRD	Aberdeen 15th c., Edinburgh 16th c.	
BIRNIE, BIRNEY	Elgin 13th c. and from MACBIRNIE	
BIRRELL, BIRREL	Berwick 15th c., Glasgow etc. 16th c.	
BIRSE, BIRSS	S. Aberdeenshire 15th c.	
BISHOP	Edinburgh 15th c., Inverness etc. 17th c.	

SURNAME	CLAN OR DISTRICT SOURCE	KEY TO MAP
BISSET, BISSETT	*FRASER*; *GRANT*	F4, G4
BLACK	From MACILDUY, *MACGREGOR*	F6
	LAMONT; *MACLEAN*	E7, D6
BLACKADDER	Merse, to Glasgow 15th c., W. Fife 18th c.	
BLACKBURN	Berwickshire etc. 13th c.	
BLACKHALL	Aberdeenshire (Garoch) 14th c.	
BLACKIE	Midlothian etc. 16th c; *LAMONT*	E7
BLACKLOCK	Dumfriesshire etc. 17th c.	
BLACKSTOCK	Dumfriesshire etc. 16th c.	
BLACKWOOD	Lanarkshire, Perth 16th c.	
BLAIKIE	From BLAKE	
BLAIN, BLANE	Wigtownshire 16th c.	
BLAIR	Ayrshire, Fife, Perthshire 13th c.;	
	GRAHAM of Menteith	I7
BLAKE, BLAIK	Berwick 13th c., Ayr 14th c.; *LAMONT*	E7
BLANCE, BLANCHE	Shetland 16th c.	
BLUE	*MACMILLAN*	D7
BLYTH, BLYTHE	Berwickshire 13th c., Dundee etc. 15th c.	
BOA, BOE	Peeblesshire 17th c., from BULLOCK	
BOAG, BOAK	Stirlingshire, Orkney etc. 16th c.	
BOATH	Angus (Both) 15th c.	
BODDIE, BODIE	Roxburghshire 13th c., Aberdeen 15th c.	
BOGIE	N. Lanarkshire 15th c.	
BOGLE	Fife, Aberdeen, Edinburgh 14th c.	
BOLD	Peeblesshire 15th c.	
BOLT	Shetland 16th c.	
BOLTON	Lothians 13th c.	
BONAR, BONNER,	Perthshire 12th c., Fife etc. 14th c.	
BONNAR	*GRAHAM* of Montrose	J5
BONE	Ayrshire, Edinburgh 17th c.	
BONNINGTON	W. Lothian, 15th c.	
BONNYMAN	Angus etc. 16th c.	
BONTEIN, BONTINE	From BUNTAIN; *GRAHAM* of Menteith	I7
BONTHRON	E. Fife 17th c.	
BOOG	Same as BOAG	
BOOKLESS	Melrose 13th c., Lothian 16th c.	
BOOTH	Aberdeen etc. 13th c.	
BORLAND	Ayrshire 16th c., Lanarkshire 17th c.	
BORROWMAN	Angus and Stirlingshire 15th c.	
BORTHWICK	Roxburghshire and Midlothian 14th c.	
BOSWALL, BOSWELL	Berwickshire 12th c., Ayrshire, Fife 14th c.	
BOTHWELL	Lanarkshire 15th c.	
BOULTON	As BOLTON	
BOURHILL	Lanarkshire 15th c.	
BOWDEN	Roxburghshire 13th c.	
BOWER, BOWERS	Peeblesshire etc. 13th c.; Angus,	
	Aberdeenshire 14th c.; *MACGREGOR*	F6
BOWIE	*MACDONALD*; *GRANT*	A4, D7, H4
BOWMAKER	E. Lothian etc. 14th c.; *MACGREGOR*	F6
BOWMAN	Aberdeen etc. 14th c.; *FARQUHARSON*	I5
BOYACK, BOWICK	Fife, Angus etc. 16th c.	
BOYCE, BOYES	Dumfriesshire etc. 12th c.; *FORBES*	J4
BOYD	Ayrshire 13th c.; *STEWART*	F7
BOYLE	Galloway 12th c.	
BOYNE	Banffshire 16th c.	
BOYTER	E. Fife, Angus 16th c.	

SURNAME	CLAN OR DISTRICT SOURCE	KEY TO MAP
BRADLEY	Hawick 13th c.	
BRAID	Midlothian 12th c.	
BRAIDWOOD	Lanarkshire 13th c.	
BRAND	Irvine 14th c., Edinburgh, Angus 16th c.	
BRASH	E.W. Stirlingshire, Edinburgh 17th c.	
BREBNER, BREMNER	Ayrshire, Moray etc. 15th c.	
BRECHIN	Angus 12th c.	
BREWER	From MACGREWAR, *DRUMMOND*	H6
BREWSTER	Lanarkshire 13th c., Aberdeen 14th c., and from MACGREWAR, *FRASER*	G4
BRIEVE	*MORRISON*	C2
BRIDGEFORD	Kincardineshire 17th c.	
BRIGGS	Speyside etc. 16th c.	
BRIMS	Caithness (Thurso) 17th c.	
BRISBANE	Aberdeenshire, Lennox, Ayrshire 14th c.	
BROCK	Dunkeld 14th c., Cromarty 16th c.	
BROCKIE	Angus, Edinburgh 15th c.	
BRODIE, BRODY	Clan *BRODIE*	H3
BRODIE	Kintyre, from Brolochan, *MACDONALD*	D7
BROGAN	Aberdeenshire (Slains) 15th c.	
BROOK, BROOKE	Aberdeen 15th c.	
BROTCHIE	Caithness, Orkney 17th c.	
BROTHERSTON	E. Lothian, Lauderdale 12th c.	
BROUGH	Perthshire and Orkney 16th c.	
BROUN, BROWN	Lanarkshire, Moray, etc. 13th c., *LAMONT*; *MACMILLAN*	E7, D7
BROW	Aberdeen 14th c., Blairgowrie 17th c.	
BROWNING	Aberdeenshire 14th c.	
BROWNLEE, BROWNLIE	Lanarkshire etc. 16th c.	
BRUCE	Clan *BRUCE*	I8, F8
BRUNTON	Mid and E. Lothian 14th c.	
BRYCE, BRICE	Stirling etc. 13th c.; *MACFARLANE*	F6
BRYDEN, BRYDON	Roxburghshire 13th c., Selkirk 16th c.	
BRYDIE, BRYDE	Perthshire 13th c.; *BRODIE*	H3
BRYSON	Clydesdale 14th c., Perthshire 15th c.	
BUCHAN	Buchan etc. 15th c.; *CUMMING*	G5
BUCHANAN	Clan *BUCHANAN*	F6
BUDGE	MACDONALD, to SINCLAIR, 15th c.	D4, I2
BUGLASS	Same as BOOKLESS	
BUIE	From Macilbowie, see BOWIE	
BUIST	Fife 16th c., Perthshire 17th c.	
BULLOCH	Peeblesshire, E. Lothian 13th c.	
BULLOCK	From BALLOCH, *MACDONALD*	D7
BUNCH	Perth 15th c.	
BUNCLE, BUNKLE	Berwickshire 12th c.; *HOME*	K7
BUNTAIN, BUNTING	Peebles 13th c., Lennox 14th c.; *GRAHAM*	I7
BUNYAN, BUNZEON	Aberdeen (Cults) to Montrose 17th c.	
BURDEN, BURDON	Merse 13th c., Perthshire, *LAMONT*	E7
BURGESS	Aberdeenshire 14th c., Orkney (from Burgar) 15th c.	
BURGOYNE, BURGON	Kinross-shire 12th c.	
BURK	*MACDONALD*	D7
BURN	Ayrshire 13th c., Angus etc. 15th c.	
BURNES, BURNESS	Renfrewshire 14th c., Angus, Ayrshire 16th c.; *CAMPBELL* of Argyll	E6
BURNET, BURNETT	Teviotdale 12th c., Deeside 14th c.	J4

SURNAME	CLAN OR DISTRICT SOURCE	KEY TO MAP
BURNIE	Dumfriesshire, from MACBIRNIE	
BURNS	From BURNESS	
BURNSIDE	Angus 16th c., Stirlingshire etc. 17th c.	
BURRELL, BURREL	Roxburghshire 12th c.	
BURT	Fife 16th c.	
BUTCHART, BUTCHER	Angus 15th c.; and from WISHART	
BUTLER	Midlothian, Perthshire etc. 13th c.	
BUTTER, BUTTERS	Perthshire 14th c.	
BUYERS, BYRES	Haddington 14th c.; *LINDSAY*	J7
CABLE	Angus 15th c.	
CADDELL, CADELL	From Cawder; *CAMPBELL*; also from	
	KETTLE, S.E. Perthshire 17th c.	H4
CADENHEAD	N. Selkirkshire 15th c.	
CADZOW	Lanarkshire (Hamilton) 13th c.	
CAIE, CAY	Aberdeenshire 16th c.	
CAIRD	Ayrshire etc. 14th c.; *MACGREGOR*	F6
CAIRNCROSS	Angus 14th c.	
CAIRNS	Mid (Calder) and W. Lothian 14th c.	
CAITHNESS	S.W. Angus (Kettins) 14th c.	
CALDER	*CAMPBELL* of Cawdor	H4
CALDERHEAD	N.E. Lanarkshire etc. 17th c.	
CALDERWOOD	Lanarkshire 13th c., Dalkeith 16th c.	
CALDWELL	Renfrewshire 14th c.	
CALLAN, CALLEN	From MACALLAN	
CALLANDER	Perthshire 14th c.; *MACFARLANE*	F6
CALLENDAR	*MACGREGOR*	F6
CALLUM	*MACGREGOR*	F6
CALLUM, CALLAM	From MACCALLUM	
CALVERT	Angus 15th c., Fife 16th c.	
CAMPBELL	*CAMPBELL* of Argyll	E6–7
CAMERON	Fife, Angus etc. 13th c.; *CAMERON*	F5
CAMBRIDGE	From MACCAMBRIDGE	
CAMPBELL	Clan *CAMPBELL* of Argyll; of Cawdor	E6, H4
	of Breadalbane; of Loudoun	G6, G7
CAMPBELL of	*MACARTHUR*	F6
STRACHUR		
CANDLISH	From MACCLANDISH	
CANNAN, CANNON	Galloway 16th c.	
CANT	W. Fife 14th c., Angus etc. 15th c.	
CANTLEY, CANTLAY	Aberdeen 15th c.	
CARGILL	Gowrie 13th c.; *DRUMMOND*	H6
CARLYLE, CARLISLE	Dumfriesshire 12th c.; *BRUCE*	I8
CARMICHAEL	Lanarkshire 13th c.; *STEWART*	H8
	Argyll, from MACMICHAEL	
CARNEGIE	Angus (Balinhard) 14th c.	J5
CARNIE	Aberdeenshire 14th c.	
CARR, CARRE	Same as *KERR*	K7
CARRICK	Ayrshire 12th c.; *KENNEDY*	F8
CARRIE	From MacHarrie, Ayrshire 15th c.	
CARRUTHERS	Annandale 13th c.; *BRUCE*	I8
CARSE, CARSS	Perth 13th c., Angus etc. 15th c.	
CARSON	From CORSANE or *MACPHERSON*	
CARSTAIRS	Lanarkshire 13th c.	
CARSWELL	Lanarkshire, Roxburghshire 13th c.	
CARTER	Kelso etc. 15th c.	

SURNAME	CLAN OR DISTRICT SOURCE	KEY TO MAP
CASH	From MACCASH	
CASKEY, CASKIE	*MACLEOD* of Lewis	C4
CASSELS	Lanarkshire etc. 17th c.	
CASSILLIS	Carrick 16th c.; *KENNEDY*	F8
CASSIE	Lanark 14th c., Aberdeen etc. 15th c.	
CATHAL, CATHIL	*MACDONALD*	C3, D7
CATHCART	Renfrewshire 12th c.	
CATHIE	*MACFIE*	C6
CATANACH	*CLAN CHATTAN*; *MACPHERSON*	G4
CATTELL	From CADDELL	
CATTO	Aberdeenshire 15th c.	
CAVEN	E. Kirkcudbrightshire (Cavens) 15th c.	
CAVERS	Roxburghshire etc. 15th c.; *DOUGLAS*	H8
CAW	From MACCAW, *STUART*	E7
CESSFORD	Roxburghshire 16th c.; *KERR*	K7
CHALMERS	Ayrshire etc. 12th c.; Aberdeenshire, *CAMERON*	F5
CHAMBERS	Lanarkshire etc. 13th c.; *CAMERON*	F5
CHAPLIN	Aberdeenshire etc. 13th c.	
CHAPMAN	Lanarkshire, Aberdeen etc. 14th c.	
CHARLES, CHARLESON	From MACKERLICH, *MACKENZIE*	F3
CHARTERS	Dumfriesshire 12th c.	
CHEAPE, CHEAP	Perth 16th c., Stirling, Kinross 17th c.	
CHERRY, CHERRIE	Ayr 14th c.	
CHEYNE, CHIENE	*CUMMING*; *SUTHERLAND*	G5, G2
CHIRNSIDE	Berwickshire 13th c.	
CHISHOLM	Clan *CHISHOLM*	F4
CHRISTIE, CHRISTY, CHRISTISON	Fife etc. 15th c.; FARQUHARSON	I5
CHRYSTAL	Ayrshire, Buchan 15th c.	
CLAPPERTON	Stirling 16th c., Stewartry 17th c.	
CLARK	*MACGREGOR*	F6
CLARK, CLARKE	*CLAN CHATTAN*; *CAMERON*	F5
	MACINTOSH; *MACPHERSON*	G4
CLARKSON, CLEARY	As CLARK, from MACCHLERY	
CLAY	From MACLAY, Appin *STEWART*	E5
CLEGHORN	Lanark 16th c.	
CLELAND, CLELLAND	Hamilton 13th c.; *MACNAB*	F6
CLEMENT	S. Perthshire etc. 15th c.; *LAMONT*	
CLEPHANE	Lauderdale 12th c., Fife 13th c.	
CLERK	Midlothian 12th c.; and as CLARK	
CLINKSCALES	Berwickshire (Coldingham) 17th c.	
CLOUSTON	Orkney (Stromness) 15th c.	
CLOW, CLOWE	Strathearn (Clow) 16th c.	
CLUNESS, CLUNIES	Beauly 14th c.; *MACKENZIE*	F3
CLUNIE, CLUNY	Gowrie 13th c.; *MACPHERSON*	G4
CLYNE	*SUTHERLAND*; *SINCLAIR*	G2, H2
COATES, COATS	From COUTTS	
COBB	Angus 15th c.; *LINDSAY*	J5
COCHRANE, COCHRAN	Paisley 13th c.; also MACEACHRAN	
COCKBURN, COBURN	Merse, to Roxburgh etc. 13th c.	J7
COGLE, COGHILL	Caithness (Wick) 17th c.	
COLES	Galloway; *MACDOUGALL*	E6
COLL	*MACDONALD*	C3, D7
COLLEDGE	Hawick etc. 17th c.	
COLLIE, COLLEY	Aberdeenshire 13th c.	
COLLIER, COLYEAR	Fife 16th c.; *ROBERTSON*	G5

SURNAME	CLAN OR DISTRICT SOURCE	KEY TO MAP
COLLINS	Angus, Aberdeen 15th c.	
COLLISON	Aberdeen 15th c.	
COLMAN	*BUCHANAN*	F6
COLQUHOUN	Clan *COLQUHOUN*	F6
COLSON	*MACDONALD*	C3, D7
COLTART, COLTHERS	Galloway 12th c.	
COLVILLE, COLVIN	Roxburghshire, Ayrshire 12th c.	G3
COMBE, COMBICH	*MACTHOMAS*; *MACINTOSH*	I5, G5
COMBIE, COMBY	Perthshire etc., Appin *STEWART*	E5
COMMON, COMMONS	Dumfriesshire; *CUMMING*	G5
COMRIE	Perthshire 15th c.; *MACGREGOR*	F6
CONACHER	*MACDOUGALL*, to *STEWART*	E6, G5
CONDIE	Strathearn (Condie) 15th c.	
CONLEY, CONLAY	From MACDONLEAVY	
CONN	Aberdeenshire, *MACDONALD*	D7
CONNAL, CONNELL	*MACDONALD*	C3–D7
CONNON	From CONN, *GORDON*	H4
CONNOCHIE, CONOCHIE	See MACCONOCHIE	
CONSTABLE	Lanarkshire 15th c.; *HAY*	I6
COOK, COOKE	Berwickshire etc. 12th c.; *MACDONALD*	D7
COOPER, COWPER	Fife (Cupar) etc. 13th c.	
COPLAND, COPELAND	Merse 12th c., Orkney, Shetland 15th c.	
CORBET, CORBETT	Teviotdale 12th c.; *ROSS*	G3
CORDINER	Aberdeen etc. 15th c.	
CORMACK	From MACCORMACK, *BUCHANAN*	F6
CORRIE, CORRY	Dumfriesshire 12th c., Ayrshire 13th c.	
CORRIGALL	Orkney (Harray) 15th c.	
CORSANE, CORSON	Galloway 12th c.	
CORSTORPHINE	Edinburgh, to E. Fife 16th c.	
COSSAR	Lanarkshire, Berwickshire 14th c.	
COTTON	Fife etc. 17th c.	
COULL	Aberdeenshire 13th c.; *MACDONALD*	C3, D7
COULSON	*MACDONALD*	C3, D7
COULTER	Lanarkshire, Aberdeenshire 13th c.	
COULTHARD	See COLTART	
COUPER, COUPAR	Fife (Cupar) etc. 13th c.	
COUSIN	Aberdeen 16th c., Fife 17th c.	
COUSLAND	Dalkeith 13th c.; *BUCHANAN*	F6
COUSTON	S.W. Angus (Couston) etc. 16th c.	
COUTIE, COUTTIE	S.W. Angus 17th c.	
COUTTS	Aberdeenshire 14th c.; *FARQUHARSON*	I5
	Angus 14th c.; *MACDONALD*	D7
COVENTRY	Berwick 13th c., Angus 14th c.	
COWAN, COWEN	From MACCOWAN: also *COLQUHOUN*	
COWE	Midlothian etc. 14th c.	
COWIE	Mearns etc. 14th c.; *FRASER*	K4
CRABB, CRABBE	Aberdeen, Berwick 14th c.	
CRAE	From *MACRAE*	E4
CRAIG	Midlothian etc. 13th c.; *GORDON*	I4
CRAIGDALLIE	*MACGREGOR*	F6
CRAIGIE	W. Lothian 12th c., Orkney 14th c.	
CRAIGMYLE	Deeside (Craigmile) 16th c.	
CRAIK	Dumfriesshire etc. 13th c.	
CRAMB, CRAM	S.W. Fife (Crombie) 12th c., Perthshire 13th c.	
CRAMOND	Edinburgh, to Angus 13th c.	

CRANE, CRAN	Angus 13th c., Aberdeenshire 14th c.	
CRANSTON	Midlothian, Roxburghshire 12th c.	J7, J8
CRAW	E. Berwickshire (Auchincraw) 14th c.	
CRAWFORD	Upper Clydesdale 12th c.; *LINDSAY*	H8, J5
CREE	Ayrshire, from *MACRAE*	E4
CRERAR, CREARER	From 'SIVEWRIGHT'; *MACINTOSH*; also *MACGREGOR*	G4, F6
CRIBBES	Lanarkshire, W. Lothian 13th c.	
CRICHTON, CRIGHTON	Midlothian (Crichton) 11th c.; Perthshire 19th c. (now a clan in its own right)	
CRIRIE	Galloway, *MACDONALD*	D7
CROALL, CROLL	Kincardineshire 13th c.	
CROCKETT, CROCKET	N. Lanarkshire 13th c., Angus etc. 15th c.	
CROMAR	Mar (Cromar), *FARQUHARSON*	I5
CROMARTY	To Orkney, 16th c., *MACKENZIE*	F3
CROMB	As CRUM; *MACDONALD* to *GORDON*	D7, I4
CROMBIE	See CRAMB; Aberdeen 16th c.; *GORDON*	J4
CROOK, CROOKES	Renfrewshire (Crookston) 12th c.	
CROSBIE	Dumfriesshire 12th c.; *BRUCE*	I8
CROW, CROWE, CROY	Perthshire etc. 15th c.; *ROSS*	G3
CROWTHER	*MACGREGOR*	F6
CROZER, CROSIER	Liddesdale 14th c.; *ARMSTRONG*	J8
CRUDEN	Aberdeenshire 15th c.	
CRUICKSHANK ⎫	E. Lothian 13th c.	
CRUICKSHANKS ⎬	Aberdeen etc. 15th c.	
CRUIKSHANK etc. ⎭	*STEWART* of Atholl	G5
CRUM, CROOM	Benderloch, *MACDONALD*	D7
CRYSTAL, CRYSTALL	See CHRYSTAL	
CUBBISON	Stewartry of Kirkcudbright 17th c.	
CUBIE, CUBBIE	Angus 15th c.	
CULBERT	Angus, Fife 16th c.	
CULCHONE	From *COLQUHOUN*	F6
CULLEN	Banffshire 14th c.; *GORDON*	J3–J4
CULLOCH	From MACCULLOCH	
CUMMING, CUMMIN, CUMMINGS, CUMYNS	Clan *CUMMING*	G5
CUNINGHAME, etc.	See CUNNINGHAM	
CUNNINGHAM	N. Ayrshire 12th c.	F7
CUNNISON	*ROBERTSON*; *MACFARLANE*	H5, F6
CURLE	Ayrshire 14th c.	
CURRER, CURROR	Berwickshire 13th c., Perth 15th c.	
CURRIE, CURREY	Annandale 12th c.; and MACVURRICH	
CURSITER	Orkney (Cursetter) 16th c.	
CUTHBERT	Lothian, Angus, Inverness 15th c.	
CUTHBERTSON	Lothian, Angus, Aberdeen 15th c.	
CUTHILL, CUTHELL	E. Lothian (Preston) 16th c.	
CUTLER	Berwickshire etc. 15th c.	
DACKER, DACRE	Aberdeen 15th c.	
DAKERS	Angus (Brechin) 16th c.	
DALGARNO	Nithsdale to Aberdeenshire 16th c.	
DALGETTY	Fife, Angus 16th c.	
DALGLEISH	Ettrickdale (Dalgleish) 15th c.	
DALLAS	Moray 13th c., *MACINTOSH*	G4
DALRYMPLE	Kyle (Dalrymple) 13th c.	
DALTON	Dumfriesshire, Aberdeen 14th c.	

SURNAME	CLAN OR DISTRICT SOURCE	KEY TO MAP
DALZIEL, DALYELL	Motherwell 13th c., Shetland 'from Yell'	H7
DANIEL, DANIELS	From DONALD, *MACDONALD*	A3—D7
DARG, DARGE	E. Lothian 15th c.; *GORDON*	J4
DARLING	Tweedside and Midlothian 14th c.	
DARROCH, DARRACH	Stirlingshire 15th c.; Renfrewshire 17th c.;	C7
	MACDONALD (now a clan in its own right)	
DAVIDSON	Clan *DAVIDSON*; *CLAN CHATTAN*	G4
DAVIE, DAVEY	Aberdeen 15th c.; *DAVIDSON*	G4
DAVIS, DAVISON,	Same as DAVIDSON	G4
DAWSON		
DAY, DEA, DEY	Banffshire 16th c.; *DAVIDSON*	G4
DEAN, DEANE	Ayrshire 15th c.; *DAVIDSON*	G4
DEANS	Hawick and Glasgow 16th c.	
DEAS, DEASON	From *DAVIDSON*	G4
DEMPSTER	Perthshire 13th c., Angus etc. 14th c.	
DENHOLM, DENHAM	Roxburghshire 13th c.	
DENNIS	Aberdeen 15th c., Linlithgow 16th c.	
DENNISON	From DENNISTON; also DENSON	
DENNISTON	Renfrewshire 13th c.; *STEWART*	F7
DENNY	Stirlingshire 15th c.	
DENOON, DENUNE	Dunoon 13th c.; *CAMPBELL*; *ROSS*	E6, G3
DENSON	Perthshire; *MACGREGOR*	
DENTON	Dumfriesshire 13th c.	
DESSON	From DAVIDSON	G4
DEUCHAR, DEUCHARS	Angus 13th c.; *LINDSAY*	J5
DEWAR	*MACNAB*; also from MACINDEOR	F6
DICK	Ayrshire etc. 15th c.	
DICKIE	Lanarkshire etc. 16th c.	
DICKSON, DICKISON	Upper Clyde etc. 14th c.; *KEITH*	K5
DINGWALL	*MUNRO*; *ROSS*	G3
DINSMORE	From DUNSMORE, *MURRAY*	H6
DINWIDDIE,	Annandale (Dinwoodie) 13th c.; *MAXWELL*	H8
DINWOODIE		
DIS, DISE	Same as DYCE	
DISHART	Fife 15th c.	
DISHINGTON	Angus 14th c., Fife 15th c.	
DIXON, DIXSON	From DICKSON	
DOBBIE, DOBIE	Peebles etc. 15th c.; *ROBERTSON*	H5
DOBBIN, DOBBINSON	Ayrshire 15th c.; *ROBERTSON*	
DOBSON, DOBIESON	Lanarkshire 15th c.; *ROBERTSON*	H5
DOCHART, DOCHERTY	Perthshire; *MACGREGOR*	F6
DODD, DODDS, DODS	Fife 13th c., E. Lothian, Sutherland 15th c.	
DOIG, DOCK	S. Perthshire, *DRUMMOND*	H6
DOLES	*MACINTOSH*	G4
DOLLAR	Clackmannanshire (Dollar) 14th c.	
DON	Aberdeenshire, Perthshire 16th c.	
DONACHIE, DONAGHY	See MACCONACHIE	
DONALD, DONALDSON	*MACDONALD*	C3—D7
DONAT, DONNAT	Perthshire 15th c.	
DONLEVY	*STEWART* of Appin	E5
DUNNACHIE	See MACCONACHIE	
DONNELL,	*MACDONALD*	C3—D7
DONNELSON		
DORREN, DORAN	Kirkcudbright 17th c.	
DORWARD, DORRAT	Mar etc. 13th c., Angus 15th c.; *GORDON*	I4
DOTT	Fife 15th c., from DODD	

SURNAME	CLAN OR DISTRICT SOURCE	KEY TO MAP
DOUGAL, DOUGALL,	*MACDOUGALL*	E6, E9
DOUGAN, DOUGHAN	Galloway etc. 17th c.	
DOUGHTIE, DOUGHTY	Peeblesshire 14th c.	
DOUGLAS, DOUGLASS	Clan *DOUGLAS*	H8, J5
	Argyllshire, from MACLUCAS	
DOULL	'Donald', Caithness 17th c.; also DOUGAL	
DOVE, DOW	*BUCHANAN*; *DAVIDSON*	F6, G4
DOWALL, DOWELL	Galloway; *MACDOUGALL*	E9
DOWIE	From MACILDOWIE	
DOWNIE	Angus 14th c.; *LINDSAY*	J5
DRAIN	From MACDRAIN	
DRENNAN, DRINNAN	Stranraer etc. 17th c.	
DREVER	Orkney 15th c.	
DREW	Stirlingshire, Glasgow 16th c.	
DRIMMIE	Gowrie (Drimmie); *MURRAY*	H6
DRUM	Deeside (Drum) 14th c.	
DRUMMOND	Clan *DRUMMOND*; Stranraer, from DRENNAN	H6
DRYBURGH	Berwickshire 13th c.	
DRYDEN	Angus 13th c.	
DRYSDALE	Annandale 15th c., to Fife 16th c.; *DOUGLAS*	H3
DUDGEON	E. Lothian 16th c.	
DUFF	*MACDUFF*; *GORDON*	I6, J4
DUFFIE, DUFFY	*MACFIE*	C6
DUFFUS, DUFFES	Moray 13th c.; *SUTHERLAND*	
DUGAL, DUGALD	*MACDOUGALL*	E6, E9
DUGUID, DUCAT	Perth etc. 14th c., Aberdeenshire 15th c.	
DUILACH	*STEWART* of Atholl	G5
DUNBAR	E. Lothian 11th c., Moray etc. 14th c.;	I3, K7,
	HOME; *MURRAY*	G2
DUNCAN, DUNCANSON	Berwick etc. 14th c.; *ROBERTSON*	G5
DUNDAS	W. Lothian 12th c.	H7
DUNLOP, DUNLAP	N. Ayrshire (Dunlop) 13th c.	
DUNN, DUN, DUNNE	Moray, Peeblesshire etc. 13th c.	
DONNACHIE	*ROBERTSON*	G5
DUNNEL	*MACDONALD*	C3–D7
DUNNET, DUNNETT	N. Caithness 16th c.	
DUNS, DUNSE	Berwickshire (Duns) 12th c.	
DUNSIRE	E. Lanarkshire (Dunsyre) 13th c.	
DUNSMORE, DUNSMURE	N. Fife (Dunsmore) 13th c.; *MURRAY*	H6
DURHAM	Dumfriesshire, Angus etc. 13th c.	
DURIE	Fife (Leven) 13th c.	
DURWARD	Same as DORWARD	
DUTHIE	Perthshire, Mearns 16th c.; *ROSS*	G3
DYCE, DYAS	Aberdeen (Dyce) 15th c.; *SKENE*	K4
DYE, DYSON	*DAVIDSON*	G4
DYER	Aberdeen etc. 14th c.	
DYKES	Lanarkshire, Perthshire 16th c.	
EADIE	Same as ADDIE; *GORDON*	J4
EANRIG, EANRUIG	*GUNN*	H2
EASDALE, etc.	See ISDALE	
EASON, EASSON	*MACKINTOSH* of Glentilt	H5
EASTON	Peeblesshire 13th c.	
EATON	From AYTON	
ECCLES	Berwickshire 12th c., Dumfriesshire 14th c.	

ECKFORD	Teviotdale (Eckford) 13th c.	
EDGAR	Nithsdale 12th c.	
EDIE, EDDIE	Same as ADDIE; *GORDON*	J4
EDINGTON	E. Berwickshire 12th c.	
EDISON	Same as ADDISON; *GORDON*	J4
EDMISTON	From EDMONSTON	
EDMOND, EDMUNDS	Aberdeen 15th c., Stirling 16th c.	
EDMONSTON	Midlothian 13th c., Roxburghshire 14th c.	
EDWARD, EDWARDS, EDWARDSON	From 'Udward'; Dumbarton and Edinburgh 15th c.	
EGGIE, EGGO	Mar 14th c.; *MACINTOSH*	H5
ELDER	Aberdeen etc. 15th c.; *MACINTOSH*	H5
ELLIOT, ELIOTT	Clan *ELLIOT*	J8
ELLIS, ELLISON	Berwickshire 13th c., Dundee 15th c.; *MACPHERSON*	G4
ELMSLIE, EMSLIE	Aberdeenshire 13th c.	
ELPHINSTONE	E. Lothian 13th c.	
ENRICK	'Eanrig', Henry: *GUNN*	H2
ERASMUSON	Shetland 17th c.	
ERSKINE	Renfrewshire 13th c., Dryburgh 16th c.	J7
ESPLIN	Stirling, Angus etc. 16th c.	
ESSLEMONT	Ythanside; *GORDON*	K4
ESSON	*MACINTOSH* of Glentilt	H5
EUNSON, EWENSON	Perthshire 13th c., Orkney 17th c.; and from MACEWAN	
EWAN	See MACEWAN	
EWART	Roxburghshire, Galloway 16th c.	
EWEN, EWING	See MACEWAN	
EWER, EWERS	See URE	
FAED	Galloway; *MACLAREN*	G6
FAICHNEY	Perthshire 16th c.	
FAIR	Border 15th c.; *ROSS*	G3
FAIRBAIRN	Lothian, Fife 12th c.; *ARMSTRONG*	J8
FAIRFOUL	Fife 15th c.	
FAIRGRIEVE	Tweedside 17th c.	
FAIRHOLM, FERME	Lanarkshire, Edinburgh 17th c.	
FAIRIE, FARIE	Ayrshire 13th c., Rutherglen 14th c.	
FAIRLEY, FAIRLIE	Ayrshire, Midlothian 14th c.; *ROSE*	H3
FAIRWEATHER	Perthshire 15th c., Angus 16th c.	
FALCONER	Kincardineshire 13th c.; *KEITH*	K5
FARMER	Fife 14th c., Perth 15th c.	
FARNINGTON	Roxburghshire (Fairnington), 13th c.	
FARQUHAR	Ayrshire 14th c.; *FARQUHARSON*	I5
FARQUHARSON	Clan *FARQUHARSON*; *CLAN CHATTAN*	I5
FAULDS	Leith 15th c., Glasgow 16th c.	
FEDERITH	*SUTHERLAND*	G2
FEE	*MACFIE*	C6
FENDER	Edinburgh 16th c., Aberdeen 17th c.	
FENTON	E. Lothian, Angus 13th c.; *CHISHOLM*	F4
FENWICK	Roxburghshire 13th c., Ayr 14th c.	
FERGUS, FERGIE	*FERGUSON*	I5
FERGUSON, FERGUSSON	Clan *FERGUSON*	I5
FERNIE, FERNEY	Cupar-Fife 14th c.	
FERRIER	E. Lothian and Angus 13th c.	
FERRIES	*FERGUSON*; *FARQUHARSON*	I5

SURNAME	CLAN OR DISTRICT SOURCE	KEY TO MAP
FERSEN	*MACPHERSON*	G4
FIDDES, FETTES	Kincardineshire 13th c., Angus 15th c.	
FIDDLER, FIDLER	Lanark 15th c., Stirling etc. 16th c	
FIFE	Fife 13th c., Aberdeen 15th c.; *MACDUFF*	I6
FINDLATER	Banffshire 14th c.; *OGILVIE*	J5
FINDLAY, FINDLAYSON, FINLAY, FINLAISON, FINLAYSON	*FARQUHARSON*	I5
FINNIE, FINNEY	Aberdeen, Glasgow etc. 16th c.	
FISHER	Perthshire 13th c., *CAMPBELL*; *MACGREGOR*	G6, F6
FISKEN	Perthshire 16th c.	
FLAWS	Orkney 15th c.	
FLEMING	Lanarkshire etc. 12th c.; *MURRAY*	H6
FLETCHER	Roxburgh and Angus 14th c.; *MACGREGOR*	F6
FLETT	Orkney 15th c.	
FLINT	Berwickshire etc. 17th c.	
FLOCKHART, FLUCKER	Fife 13th c.	
FOGGO, FOGO	Merse 12th c.; Aberdeen, Foggie	
FOOT, FOOTE	Angus 15th c.	
FORBES	Clan *FORBES*	J4, K3
FORD, FOORD	Annandale etc. 15th c.	
FORDYCE	Banffshire 15th c.; *FORBES*	J4
FOREST	Tweeddale etc. 14th c.; *DOUGLAS*	H8
FORGIE	*FERGUSON*	I5
FORMAN, FOREMAN	Midlothian 13th c., Tweedside 15th c.	
FORREST	From FOREST, also FORRESTER	
FORRESTER	Stirlingshire 12th c.; *MACDONALD*	D7
FORSON	Melrose 17th c.	
FORSTER, FOSTER	From FORRESTER	
FORSYTH	Edinburgh, Stirling 14th c.; *LAMONT*	E7
FORTUNE	E. Lothian 13th c.	
FOTHERINGHAM	Angus 13th c.; *LINDSAY*	J5
FOUBISTER	Orkney 16th c.	
FOULIS, FOWLIS	Perthshire etc. 13th c.; *MUNRO*	G3
FOWLER	Berwickshire, Edinburgh 14th c.	
FOX	Kelso 16th c., Angus 17th c.	
FRAME, FRAM	N. Lanarkshire etc. 15th c.	
FRANCIS, FRANCE	Dumfriesshire 12th c.; *STEWART*	F7
FRASER, FRAZER	Clan *FRASER*	G4, F4, K3, K4
FRATER	Kelso 16th c.	
FREEMAN	Peeblesshire 13th c.	
FRENCH	Annandale, Lothian etc. 13th c.	
FRESER, FREZEL	Same as *FRASER*	
FREW	S. Perthshire 16th c.	
FRIER, FREER	Berwickshire etc. 13th c.	
FRISELL, FRIZELLE	Same as *FRASER*	
FULLARTON, FULLERTON	Ayrshire 13th c.; *STUART* of Bute	E7
FULTON	Ayrshire, Lanarkshire 13th c.	
FURMAGE	Dundee 13th c.	
FUTHIE	Angus, Aberdeen 14th c.; *OGILVIE*	J5
FYALL	Fife 16th c.	
FYFE, FYFFE	See FIFE	
GAIR	E. Ross 16th c.; *GAYRE*; *ROSS*; *MACGREGOR*	G3, F6
GAIRN, GAIRNS	Angus, from GARDEN; also *GAYRE*	

SURNAME	CLAN OR DISTRICT SOURCE	KEY TO MAP
GALBRAITH ⎫ GALBREATH ⎰	Lennox 12th c. *MACFARLANE*; *MACDONALD*	G7 F6, D7
GALL, GAUL	See GALT	
GALLETLY	Perth, Aberdeen 13th c.	
GALLIE	Ayrshire 15th c.; *GUNN*	H2
GALLOWAY	To Atholl 13th c.; *MACFARLANE*	F6
GALT	Perth 14th c., Aberdeen 15th c., Ayrshire 17th c.; *MACDONALD*	D7
GANSON, GAUNSON	Nairn 13th c.; *GUNN*	H2
GARDEN, GARDYNE	Angus and Midlothian 13th c.	
GARDINER, GARDNER	Perthshire etc. 15th c.; *GORDON*	J4
GARLAND	Perthshire 13th c.	
GARIOCH, GARRICK, GARRIOCK, GERRIE	Aberdeenshire, Midlothian 13th c., Shetland 15th c.; *GORDON*	J4
GARRATT, GARRETT	Glasgow 16th c., from GERARD	
GARRISON, GARSON	*GAYRE*	
GARROW	Perthshire, see MACGARROW	
GARVIE	Gowrie, Angus 16th c.; MACGARVIE	
GAULD, GAULT	Same as GALT	
GAULDIE, GALDIE	Same as GALLIE	
GAVIN, GAVINE	Angus, Border etc. 17th c.	
GAY	Angus 15th c., Fife etc. 17th c.	
GAYRE	Clan *GAYRE*	
GEAR	Shetland 17th c., from GAIR; *GAYRE*; *ROSS*	G3
GEDDES	*ROSE*, to *SCOTT* 15th c.; *GORDON*	H3, I8, I4
GEDDIE	Angus (Glamis) 14th c.	
GEEKIE, GEIKIE	S. Angus (Gagie) 15th c.	
GEIR	*GAYRE*	
GELLATLY	Perth, Aberdeen 13th c.	
GEMMELL	E. Lothian, Tweed 13th c., Carrick 16th c.	
GEORGE	Ayrshire 15th c.	
GEORGESON	Angus 15th c.; *GUNN*	H2
GERARD, GERRARD	Annandale 12th c., Aberdeenshire 16th c.	
GIBB, GIBBON	From GILBERT	
GIBSON	Fife, Midlothian 13th c.; *BUCHANAN*; *CAMERON*	F6, F5
GIFFORD	E. Lothian 12th c.; *HAY*	J7
GILBERT	Bute etc. 14th c., *BUCHANAN*	F6
GILBERTSON	Peeblesshire 13th c.; *BUCHANAN*; *CAMERON*	F6, F5
GILBRIDE	*MACDONALD*	C3–D7
GILCHRIST	*MACLACHLAN*; *OGILVIE*	E6, J5
GILES	Lanarkshire 13th c., Dunbartonshire 16th c.	
GILFILLAN	Stirlingshire, *MACNAB*	F6
GILL	Perth etc. 14th c.; *MACDONALD*	D7
GILLAM	'William', S. Perthshire 17th c.	
GILLAN, GILLAND	From GILLIAN; also GILLILAND	
GILLANDERS	Kincardineshire 13th c.; *ROSS*	G3
GILLESPIE	Lennox 12th c.; *MACPHERSON*	G4
GILLIAN, GILLON	'Gil'lan'; *MACLEAN*	D6
GILLIES, GILLIE	Lothian 12th c.; *MACPHERSON*	G4
GILLILAND	From MACLELLAND; Ayrshire 17th c.	
GILMORE, GILMOUR	Clackmannan etc. 12th c.; *MORRISON*	C2
GILRAY, GILVRAY	From *MACGILLIVRAY*	
GILROY	From MACILROY	
GILRUTH	From MACILRIACH; *FRASER*	K4
GILZEAN	From GILLIAN, *MACLEAN*	D6

SURNAME	CLAN OR DISTRICT SOURCE	KEY TO MAP
GIRDWOOD	Lanarkshire (Carnwarth) 16th c.	
GLADSTONE	Clydesdale 13th c., Teviotdale 14th c.	
GLAISTER	Angus (Glaister) 13th c.	
GLASS	Bute etc. 15th c.; *STUART* of Bute	E7
GLASSFORD	Mid Lanarkshire 13th c.	
GLEGG	Angus and Mearns 17th c.	
GLEN	Peeblesshire (Traquair) 14th c.	
GLENDINNING	E. Dumfriesshire 13th c.; *DOUGLAS*	H8
GLENNIE, GLENNY	Braemar 14th c., *MACINTOSH*	G4
GLOAG	Perthshire 16th c.	
GLOVER	Perth 13th c., Glasgow etc. 16th c.	
GOLD, GOOLD	Angus 13th c.	
GOLDIE	Galloway etc. 16th c.	
GOLLAN	Kinross-shire 13th c.	
GOOD	Ayr, Glasgow etc. 16th c.	
GOODAL	Roxburghshire 13th c.	
GOODFELLOW	Angus 15th c., Lanark etc. 17th c.	
GOODLAD, GOODLET	Stirling 14th c., Fife 15th c., Shetland 16th c.	
GOODSIR, GOODYEAR	E. Fife 14th c.; also *MACGREGOR*	F6
GOODWILLIE	Fife 12th c.	
GORDON	Clan *GORDON*	I4, J4, K4
GORRIE, GORRY	Perthshire 16th c.; *MACDONALD*	C3−D7
GOUDIE, GOULDIE	Edinburgh, Shetland, Ayrshire 16th c.; *MACPHERSON*	G4
GOULD	Perthshire 17th c., from GOLD	
GOURLAY, GOURLEY	Midlothian, Fife etc. 12th c.	
GOVAN	Glasgow, to Peeblesshire 13th c.	
GOW	Fife etc. 16th c.; *MACPHERSON*	G4
GOWAN, GOWANS	*MACDONALD*; Perthshire, *MACPHERSON*	D7, G4
GRACIE	From GREUSACH via Grassick	
GRAHAM, GRAHAME	Clan *GRAHAM*	I7, J5, G5
GRAINGER, GRANGER	Roxburgh, Edinburgh etc. 13th c.	
GRANT	Clan *GRANT*	H4, F4
GRASSICK	From GREUSACH	
GRAY	Fife etc. 13th c.; *SUTHERLAND*	G2
	From MACGLASHAN, *STEWART*	G5
GREEN	Roxburghshire 13th c., Moray etc. 15th c.	
GREENLAW	Berwickshire 12th c.; *HOME*	K7
GREENLEES	Lanarkshire (Cambuslang) 16th c.	
GREER	*MACGREGOR*	F6
GREGG	*MACGREGOR*	F6
GREGOR, GREGORY	Fife 14th c.; *MACGREGOR*	F6
GREGORSON, GREGSON	*MACGREGOR*	F6
GREIG	Fife 13th c.; *MACGREGOR*	F6
GREUSACH	Aberdeenshire; *FARQUHARSON*	I5
GREWAR	See MACGREWAR	
GREY	Same as GRAY	
GREYSON	From GRIERSON; *MACGREGOR*	F6
GRIERSON, GRIER	Dumfriesshire 14th c.; *MACGREGOR*	F6
GRIESCK	*MACFARLANE*	F6
GRIEVE, GREIVE	Berwickshire 13th c., Aberdeen etc. 14th c.	
GRIFFIN	Angus and Moray 13th c.	
CRIGG	*MACGREGOR*	F6
GRIGOR	Aberdeenshire etc.; *MACGREGOR*	F6
GRIMMOND	Perthshire, from MACCRIMMON	
GRINTON	Peeblesshire, W. Lothian 16th c.	

SURNAME	CLAN OR DISTRICT SOURCE	KEY TO MAP
GROAT	Caithness 15th c.; *SINCLAIR*	I2
GROUNDWATER	Orkney 17th c.	
GROZIER	From CROSIER; *ARMSTRONG*	J8
GRUAMACH	*MACFARLANE*	F6
GRUAR, GRUER	See MACGREWAR	
GRUBB	Angus (Brechin) 17th c.	
GUDGER	*MACGREGOR*	F6
GUILD	Stirling, Angus, Perthshire 15th c.	
GUINNESS	*MACGREGOR*	F6
GULLAND, GULLEN	E. Lothian (Gullane) 12th c.	
GUNN	Clan *GUNN*	H2
GUTHRIE	Angus (Guthrie) 13th c.	

HADDEN, HADDON	Kelso, to Perthshire 12th c.; *GRAHAM*	G6
HADDOW	Lanarkshire etc. 17th c.	
HAGGART, HAGART	Perthshire 16th c.; *ROSS*	G3
HAIG	Berwickshire 12th c.	
HAIR, HARE	Ayrshire, Edinburgh 14th c.	
HALCROW	Orkney 15th c.	
HALDANE, HALDEN	Same as HADDEN	
HALKETT, HACKETT	Ayrshire and Fife 13th c.	
HALIBURTON	Merse 12th c., to Angus 13th c.; *HOME*	J7
HALL	Renfrewshire and Fife 14th c.	
HALLEY, HALLY	Orkney 16th c., Perthshire 17th c.	
HALLIDAY	Dumfriesshire 14th c.	
HAMILTON	Renfrewshire 13th c.	G7, E8
HANDYSIDE	Berwick 14th c.	
HANNAH, HANNAY	Wigtownshire 13th c.	
HANNAN	Kirkcudbrightshire 17th c.	
HANNING	Berwick 12th c., Dumfriesshire etc. 17th c.	
HARCUS	Merse (Harcarse) 13th c., Orkney 16th c.	
HARDIE, HARDY	Lanarkshire 13th c., and MACHARDIE	
HARKESS, HARKES	Same as HARCUS	
HARKNESS	Dumfriesshire 16th c.	
HARPER	Lanarkshire etc. 13th c.; *BUCHANAN*	F6
HARPERSON	From MACCHRUITER	
HARRISON	Aberdeen 14th c., Fife 15th c., Shetland 17th c.	
HARROLD, HAROLD	Orkney 15th c., *MACLEOD*	C4
HARROWER	E. Fife 14th c., Perth etc. 15th c.	
HART, HARTE	Lanarkshire 13th c.	
HARVEY, HARVIE	Aberdeen etc. 14th c.; *KEITH*	K4
HASTIE	Menteith 14th c., Border 16th c.	
HASTINGS	N.E. Angus (Dun) 12th c.	
HASTON	Galloway (Heston I.) 17th c.	
HASWELL	Berwickshire 12th c.	
HAWES, HAWS	*CAMPBELL*	E6
HAWSON	Tweedside 15th c.; *CAMPBELL*	E6
HAWICK	Roxburghshire 12th c.	
HAWTHORN	Galloway 15th c.; *MACDONALD*	D7
HAXTON	Mearns (Halkerston) 13th c.; *KEITH*	J5
HAY	Clan *HAY*	I6, K4
HEATLIE, HEATLY	Tweedside 13th c.	
HEDDELL, HEDDLE	Orkney 14th c.	
HEDDERWICK	Dunbar 15th c.; also Arbroath 16th c.	
HEGGIE	From MACKEGGIE; *MACINTOSH*	H5

SURNAME	CLAN OR DISTRICT SOURCE	KEY TO MAP
HENDERSON	Aberdeen and Liddesdale 14th c.; *GUNN* From MACHENRY	H2
HENDRIE, HENDRY, HENRY, HENDERY	Ayrshire etc. 16th c.; and from MACHENRY	
HEPBURN	E. Lothian 14th c.	
HERBERT	Stirlingshire 13th c.	
HERBERTSON	Glasgow and E. Lothian 16th c.	
HERD	Angus and Galloway 14th c.	
HERDMAN	Aberdeenshire etc. 15th c.	
HERIOT, HERRIOT	Midlothian 12th c., to Glasgow etc. 16th c.	
HERKES, HERKIS	Same as HARCUS	
HERMISTON	Roxburghshire 12th c., to E. Ross etc. 14th c.	
HERON	Stewartry 12th c.; also MACKERRON	
HERRIES	Dumfriesshire 13th c., Galloway 14th c.	
HERVEY	Same as HARVEY	
HEWISON	*MACDONALD*	A3—D7
HEWITT, HEWAT	Aberdeen 15th c., Berwickshire 17th c.	
HIGGINSON	From MACKEGGIE; *MACINTOSH*	H5
HIGHET, HIGHGATE	Glasgow 16th c.	
HILL	Roxburghshire 13th c., Aberdeen etc. 14th c.	
HISLOP, HESLOP	Edinburgh and Lanarkshire 15th c.	
HOBKIRK	Hawick (Hopekirk), to Midlothian 16th c.	
HOBSON	*ROBERTSON*	G5
HODGE, HODGES	From ROGER; Glasgow etc. 15th c.	
HOGARTH, HOGGART	Fife 15th c., Roxburghshire 17th c.	
HOGG, HOG, HOGGE	Berwickshire, Edinburgh etc. 13th c.	
HOLLAND	Orkney, Angus, Ayrshire 15th c.	
HOLLIDAY	From HALLIDAY	
HOLMES	Ayrshire 15th c.; and from *HOME*	
HOME	Clan *HOME*	K7
HONEYMAN	Fife 15th c., Orkney 17th c.	
HOOD	Midlothian and Moray, 13th c.	
HOOK	Dumfriesshire 13th c.	
HOPE	Lanarkshire etc. 13th c., Lothian 16th c.	H7
HOPKIRK	See HOBKIRK	
HORN, HORNE	Dumfriesshire 14th c., Aberdeen etc. 15th c.	
HORNER	Angus 15th c., Glasgow 16th c.	
HORSBURGH	Peebles 13th c.	
HOSSACK, HOSICK	Beauly Firth 16th c.; *MACINTOSH*	G4
HOULISTON	Midlothian (Heriot) 13th c.	
HOUSTON, HOUSTOUN	Renfrewshire 12th c.; *MACDONALD* Caithness, from OGSTOUN	D4
HOWATT, HOWITT	Aberdeen 15th c., Angus 17th c.; *MACDONALD*	D4
HOWDEN	Same as HADDEN	
HOWE, HOW, HOWIE	Angus and Ayrshire 16th c.; *MACDONALD*	D4
HOWELL, HOWELLS	From MACHOWELL, *MACDOUGALL*	E9
HOWIESON, HUGHSON	Aberdeenshire etc. 14th c.; *MACDONALD*	D4
HOY	Roxburghshire, Orkney 17th c.	
HUDSON, HUTSON	Kelso 15th c.; also from HUTCHON	
HUGGAN	Fife, Lauderdale 16th c.; Bute 17th c.	
HUIE	From MACILDOWIE, *MACLEAN*	D6
HUME	Same as *HOME*; *MACDUFF*	K7, I6
HUNNAM, HOUNAM	E. Roxburghshire (Hownam) 12th c.	
HUNTER, HUNT	Peeblesshire, Ayrshire etc. 13th c., Stronsay (Hunto) 16th c.; *STUART*	E7
HUNTLY	Berwickshire 13th c.; *GORDON*	I4

HURRY, HURRIE	Kincardineshire (Urrie) 13th c.; *KEITH*	J5
HUSBAND	Nairn 13th c., Perth 16th c.	
HUTCHEON, HUTCHIN	See HUTCHON	
HUTCHESON, HUTCHINSON, HUTCHISON	Glasgow, Aberdeen etc. 15th c.; *MACDONALD*	D4
HUTCHON, HUTSON	Aberdeen etc. 15th c.; *MACDONALD*	D4
HUTTON	Lanark 13th c., Fife 15th c.	
HYND, HYNDE	Glasgow etc. 15th c.	
HYNDFORD	Lanark 13th c.	
HYNDMAN	Renfrewshire 16th c.	
HYSLOP	See HISLOP	
IMLACH, IMLAH	Aberdeenshire 15th c.	
IMRIE, IMERY	S. Perthshire 15th c., Fife 16th c.	
INCH	W. Fife 13th c., Angus 15th c.; *INNES*	I3
INCHES	Perthshire; *ROBERTSON*	G5
INGLIS, INGLES	Lanarkshire etc. 13th c.; *DOUGLAS*	H8
INGRAM	Angus 14th c.; *COLQUHOUN*	F6
INKSTER	Orkney 15th c., Shetland 16th c.	
INNES	Clan *INNES*	I3
INRIG	Caithness 17th c., see ENDRICK	
INVERARITY	Angus 17th c.	
IRELAND	Perthshire 13th c., Orkney 14th c.	
IRONS	Angus 15th c.	
IRONSIDE	Aberdeenshire 16th c.	
IRVINE, IRVING, IRWIN, IRVIN	Dumfriesshire, Ayrshire 12th c.; Deeside 14th c., Shetland 16th c.	J4, 5
ISAAC, ISAACS	See MACISAAC	
ISBISTER	Orkney (Harray) 16th c.	
ISDALE, EASDALE	Border 'Eskdale' to Ayrshire 15th c.	
ISLES	*MACDONALD*	C3–D7
IVERACH, IVORY	From MACIVER, *MACKENZIE*	F3
IVERSON	Same as MACIVER	
IZATT, IZZETT	W. Fife, Ayrshire 16th c.	
JACK	Angus and Lanarkshire 15th c.	
JACKSON	Aberdeen, Glasgow etc. 15th c.	
JACOB, JACOBS	Angus 14th c.	
JAFFREY	Aberdeenshire 16th c., from JEFFREY	
JAMESON, JAMIESON	*GUNN*; (Maccamie); *STUART*	H2, E7
JAMIE	W. Lothian 16th c., Lanarkshire etc. 17th c.	
JARDINE	Angus 12th c., Dumfriesshire 13th c.	
JARVIS, JARVIE	Angus, Stirling etc. 16th c.	
JEFFERIES, JEFFERS, JEFFERSON, JEFFERY	From 'Geoffrey', Peeblesshire etc. 13th c., Angus, Aberdeen 14th c.; *MACDONALD*	D7
JENKIN, JENKINS	Moray, Lanarkshire etc. 16th c.	
JERRAT, JARRETT	See GARRATT	
JENNER	Berwickshire 13th c., Inverness 15th c.	
JERDAN	From JARDINE	
JERVIS	From 'Gervase', see JARVIS	
JESSIMAN	Aberdeenshire 16th c.; *GORDON*	I4
JOBSON, JOPSON	Annandale 14th c., Edinburgh etc. 17th c.	
JOHNSON	*GUNN*; also from MACIAN	
JOHNSTON	Clan *JOHNSTON*; also *MACGREGOR*	I8, F6

SURNAME	CLAN OR DISTRICT SOURCE	KEY TO MAP
JOHNSTONE	As *JOHNSTON*; Coll, *MACDONALD* of Ardnamurchan	I8, D5
JOLLIE, JOLLY	Kincardineshire 14th c.	
JOPP	Perth 14th c., Huntly 16th c.; *GORDON*	J4
JORDAN	Aberdeen 13th c.	
JOSS	Fife 14th c., Aberdeenshire 16th c.	
JUDGE	Perthshire 13th c.; *MORRISON*	C2
JUDSON	Edinburgh 14th c.	
JUNER, JUNOR	Inverness, from JENNER	
JUSTICE	Perthshire and Angus 15th c.	
KAY, KEAY	Aberdeen etc. 14th c.; *DAVIDSON*	G4
	From MACKAY	F2
KEAN, KEENE	From MACIAN	
KEDDIE	Fife etc. 16th c., from MACADIE	
KEEGAN	From MACKEEGAN, *MACDONALD*	A3
KEIGHREN	From MACEACHRAN	
KEILLER, KEILOR	Angus, Perth, Mar 13th c.	
KEIR	Stirlingshire 13th c., Ayrshire 16th c.	
KEITH	Clan *KEITH*	K5, K4, K3
	MACPHERSON; *SUTHERLAND*	G4, G2
KELDAY	Orkney (Keldall) 16th c.	
KELLAR, KELLER	From KEILLER; also MACKELLAR	
KELLAS	Moray, *FARQUHARSON*	I5
KELLOCK	Stirling 14th c., Fife 15th c.	
KELLY, KELLIE	Galloway 12th c., Angus 14th c.; *MACDONALD*	C5
KELMAN	Aberdeenshire 16th c.	
KELTIE, KELTY	Callander (Keltic), to Edinburgh 17th c.	
KEMP	Edinburgh 15th c., Dingwall 16th c.	
KENNAWAY	Fife (Kennoway), to W. Lothian 17th c.	
KENNEDY	Clan *KENNEDY*; Lochaber, *CAMERON*	F8, F5
KENNETH, KENNETHSON	*MACKENZIE*	F3
KENRICK, KENDRICK	From MACKENDRICK	
KENT	E. Lothian 12th c., Fife 16th c.	
KEPPIE	Fife 17th c.	
KER, KERR	Clan *KERR*	K7
KERMACK	Buchan (Kermuck) 14th c.	
KERRACHER	MACERRACHER, *FARQUHARSON*	I5
KESSAN, KESSEN	Lennox 14th c., Ayr etc. 16th c.	
KETCHEN, KETCHIN	*MACDONALD* of Clanranald	D5
KETTLE, KETTLES	S.E. Perthshire 13th c.	
KEY, KEYS	Same as KAY	
KID, KIDD	Lanarkshire 12th c., Angus 14th c.	
KIDDIE	Same as KEDDIE	
KILGOUR	N.W. Fife, to Aberdeen 16th c.; *MACDUFF*	I6
KILPATRICK	Same as KIRKPATRICK	
KINCAID	S. Stirlingshire (Kincaid) 15th c. (now a clan in its own right)	
KING	Aberdeenshire 13th c., Berwickshire etc. 15th c.; and from MACAREE	
KINGHORN	Fife, to Lothian etc. 13th c.	
KININMONTH	Fife 12th c.	
KINLOCH	N.W. Fife (Kinloch-Rossie) 12th c.	
KINNAIRD	Perthshire (Gowrie) 12th c.	
KINNEAR	Fife (Wormit) 12th c.	

SURNAME	CLAN OR DISTRICT SOURCE	KEY TO MAP
KINNELL	Angus 14th c.; Fife 17th c.; *MACDONALD*	D7
KINNIESON	See CUNNISON	
KINROSS	Kinross 12th c.	
KIRK	Perth, Arbroath 15th c., Dumfriesshire 17th c.	
KIRKALDY	Fife (Kirkcaldy) 17th c.	
KIRKBY	Berwickshire 13th c.	
KIRKLAND	Merse 13th c., Glasgow etc. 15th c.	
KIRKNESS	Orkney 14th c., Shetland 15th c.	
KIRKPATRICK	Nith 12th c.; *DOUGLAS*; *COLQUHOUN*	H8, F6
KIRKWOOD	Stirling 15th c., Ayrshire 16th c.; *MACGREGOR*	F6
KISSACK, KISSOCK	Moray, from MACISAAC	
KNIGHT	Angus 14th c., Dumfries etc. 16th c.	
KNOWLES, KNOX	Aberdeenshire (Deer) 15th c.	
KNOX	Renfrewshire 13th c.; *MACFARLANE*	F6
KYD, KYDD	Same as KIDD	
KYLE	Ayrshire (Kyle) 15th c.	
KYNOCH	*ROBERTSON*; *MACKENZIE*	H5, F3
LACHLAN, LACHIE	*MACLACHLAN*	E6
LACKIE	Angus, from LECKIE	
LAIDLAW, LAIDLAY	Selkirkshire 13th c.; *SCOTT*	I8
LAIKIE	*MACGREGOR*	F6
LAING	Dumfries 14th c., Glasgow 15th c.; *GORDON*;	I4
	COLQUHOUN; *MACDONALD*	F6, D7
LAIRD	Berwick and Peeblesshire 13th c.	
LAMB	Merse 13th c., Leith etc. 14th c.; *LAMONT*	E7
LAMBERT	E. Fife 13th c.	
LAMBIE, LAMMIE	From LAMB, Angus 13th c.; *LAMONT*	E7
LAMONDSON	*LAMONT*	E7
LAMONT, LAMOND	Clan *LAMONT*	E7
LANDALE, LANDELLS, LANDELS	Roxburghshire, E. Lothian 12th c.; *HOME*	J7
LANE	Angus, Aberdeen 16th c.	
LANG	Berwickshire 13th c., Aberdeen 14th c.;	I4, D7
	GORDON; *MACDONALD*	
LANGLANDS	Peeblesshire 14th c.; *SCOTT*	I8
LARNACH	Lorne, to Caithness etc.; *MACLAREN*	G6
LARNACK	Lorne, to *STEWART* of Atholl	H5
LATIMER	Dumfriesshire 14th c.	
LATTA, LATTO	Ayrshire (Laithes) 14th c.	
LAUCHLAN	*MACLACHLAN*	E6
LAUDER	Lauderdale 13th c.	J7
LAURENCE	Biggar 13th c., Aberdeen 16th c.; *MACLAREN*	G6
LAURENSON	Fife 15th c., Shetland 16th c.; *MACLAREN*	G6
LAURIE	Galloway etc. 16th c.; *GORDON*	J4
LAW	Glasgow etc. 15th c.; *MACLAREN*	G6
LAWRENCE, LAWRIE	See LAURENCE, LAURIE	
LAWSON	Midlothian 14th c.; *MACLAREN*	G6
LAWTHER	See LAUDER	
LEACH	See LEITCH	
LEADBETTER	W. Lothian 14th c.	
LEAN	From *MACLEAN*	B5
LEAPER	Edinburgh 12th c., Buchan 13th c.; NAPIER	
LEARMONTH	Berwickshire (Earlston) 11th c.	
LEARY	From MACLEARY	
LEASK	Buchan (Leask) 14th c., Orkney 15th c.	

LEAVY	From MACDONLEAVY	
LEAY	From MACLEAY	
LECKIE, LECKY	Stirlingshire 14th c.; *MACGREGOR*	F6
LEDINGHAM	Aberdeenshire 16th c.	
LEE	Lanark 12th c.	
LEES, LEESON	From MACLEES	
LEGG, LEGGE	Dumfriesshire 13th c., Banffshire 16th c.	
LEGGAT, LEGGET	Stirling etc. 15th c.	
LEIGHTON	Fife and Angus 13th c.	
LEIPER, LEIPPER	See LEAPER	
LEISHMAN	Lanarkshire 15th c., Stirlingshire 16th c.	
LEISK	Same as LEASK	
LEITCH, LEETCH	Aberdeen, Glasgow etc. 14th c.; *MACBETH*; *MACDONALD*	I3, D7
LEITH	Lothian and Aberdeenshire 14th c.	
LEITHEAD	Midlothian and Border 17th c.	
LEMMON, LEMOND	From LAMONT	E7
LENG	From LANG	
LENNIE, LENNY	Perthshire (Leny) 13th c.; *BUCHANAN*	F6
LENNOX	Lennox 12th c.; *MACFARLANE*	G7, F6
LENNOX	*STEWART*	F7
LESLIE, LESSLIE	Clan *LESLIE*	J4, I3
LESSELS	'Lascelles', Fife etc. 12th c.	
LETHAM, LETHEM	Berwickshire and Angus 13th c.	
LEUCHARS, LEURS	Fife (Leuchars) 14th c.	
LEVACK	Caithness 17th c.; Appin *STEWART*	E5
LEWIS	Bute, *STUART*; *MACLEOD*	E7, C2
LIDDELL, LIDDLE	Roxburghshire 13th c., Aberdeen 14th c.	
LIGHTBODY	N. Lanarkshire 16th c., W. Lothian 17th c.	
LILBURN	Aberdeen 15th c.	
LILLICO	Roxburghshire 17th c.	
LILLIE, LILLY	Peeblesshire 13th c.	
LIMOND, LIMONT	From *LAMONT*	E7
LIND, LINE	From LYNN	
LINDORES	Fife, Aberdeen etc. 15th c.	
LINDSAY	Clan *LINDSAY*	J5—J7
LINKLATER	Orkney 15th c.	
LILLE, LILE	Same as LYLE	
LISTER	From LITSTER	
LISTON	W. Lothian (Liston) 12th c.	
LITHGOW	Linlithgow, to Berwick etc. 13th c.	
LITSTER	Perth, Lothians etc. 13th c.	
LITTLE	Angus 13th c., to Dumfriesshire etc. 14th c.	
LITTLEJOHN	Aberdeen and Glasgow 15th c.	
LIVINGSTON, LIVINGSTONE	W. Lothian 12th c.; From MACLEAY; Appin *STEWART*; *MACDOUGALL*	E5, E6
LOBBAN	Nairn 16th c.; *MACLENNAN*	E4
LOCH	Peeblesshire 13th c.	
LOCHHEAD	Lanarkshire, Aberdeenshire 13th c.	
LOCKE, LOCK	Roxburghshire 13th c., Glasgow etc. 16th c.	
LOCKERBY	Lockerbie (place), *DOUGLAS*	H8
LOCKHART	Ayrshire, Lanarkshire 12th c.	
LOCKIE	Angus and Midlothian 16th c.	
LOGAN	Ayrshire, Fife etc. 13th c.; *MACLENNAN*	E4
LOGIE, LOGGIE	Fife etc. 13th c.	
LONGMUIR	Ayrshire and Midlothian 13th c.	

SURNAME	CLAN OR DISTRICT SOURCE	KEY TO MAP
LONIE	From MACGILLONIE, *CAMERON*	F5
LORIMER	Perthshire 12th c., Midlothian 15th c.	
LORNE	Appin *STEWART*; *CAMPBELL*	E5, E6
LORNIE	Gowrie 13th c., *HAY*	I6
LORRAINE	Berwickshire 13th c.	
LOTHIAN	Lothian, Berwick 14th c., Angus etc. 15th c.	
LOUDEN, LOUDON	Ayrshire (Loudoun) 12th c.; *CAMPBELL*	G7
	Fife 16th c. (from LOTHIAN)	
LOURIE, LOWRIE	Same as LAURIE	
LOUTIT, LOUTTIT	Strathearn 12th c., to Orkney 15th c.	
LOVE	Dundee 13th c., Glasgow 15th c.; *MACKINNON*	D4
LOVEL, LOVELL	Roxburghshire 12th c., Angus 13th c.	
LOW, LOWE	Perthshire 14th c., Angus 15th c.; *MACLAREN*	G6
LOWDEN, LOWDON	See LOUDEN	
LOWSON	Aberdeen 14th c.; *MACLAREN*	G6
LOY	From MACCLOY, *STUART*	E7
LUCAS, LUCKIE	From MACLUCAS	
LUGTON	Midlothian, to Fife 16th c.	
LUKE, LUCK	From MACLUCAS, *LAMONT*	E7
LUMBARD, LOMBARD	Renfrewshire 13th c.; *STEWART*	F7
LUMGAIR	Kincardineshire 13th c.; *KEITH*	K5
LUMLEY	Lanark 14th c.	
LUMSDEN ⎱	Berwickshire 12th c., Fife 14th c.	
LUMSDAINE ⎰	Aberdeenshire 14th c.; *FORBES*	J4
LUNAN	Angus and Aberdeenshire 14th c.	
LUNDIE, LUNDIN	Fife and Angus 12th c.	
LUNN, LUND	Berwickshire, Angus etc. 16th c.	
LYALL, LYELL	Angus 14th c.; *SINCLAIR*	I2
LYLE	Renfrewshire 12th c.; *STEWART*	F7
LYNE, LYNN	Ayrshire and Perth 13th c.	
LYON	Perthshire 12th c.; *FARQUHARSON*	I5
MABEN, MABON	Dumfriesshire etc. 17th c.	
MACACHIN	*MACDONALD* of Clanranald	D5
MACACHOUNICH	*COLQUHOUN*	F6
MACADAM	Angus 15th c., Ayrshire 16th c.; *MACGREGOR*	F6
MACADIE	*FERGUSON*; *MUNRO*	I5, G3
MACAICHAN	*MACDONALD* of Clanranald	D5
MACADOO	Galloway 17th c.	
MACAINDRA	*MACFARLANE*	F6
MACAINSH	See MACANISH	
MACALASTER	(Same as FLETCHER), *MACGREGOR*	F6
MACALDONICH	*BUCHANAN*	F6
MACALDOWIE, MACALDUIE	See MACILDOWIE	
MACALEAR	Galloway, from MACCLURE	
MACALEERIE	Galloway, from MACCHLERY	
MACALEES	Galloway, from MACLEES	
MACALESTER	*MACALISTER*; *MACGREGOR*	D7, F6
MACALISTER	Clan *MACALISTER*	D7
MACALL	See MACCALL	
MACALLAN	Aberdeenshire 17th c., *MACFARLANE*	F6
	Clanranald *MACDONALD*; *GRANT*	D5, H4
	MACKAY; Kirkcudbrightshire 14th c.	F2
MACALLASTER	*MACALISTER*	D7
MACALLEY	From *MACAULAY*	

SURNAME	CLAN OR DISTRICT SOURCE	KEY TO MAP
MACALLISTER	*MACALISTER*	D7
MACALLUM	From *MACCALLUM*	
MACALMAN	From MACCALMAN, *BUCHANAN*	F6
MACALONIE	From MACGILLONIE, *CAMERON*	F5
MACALPIN, MACALPINE	Clan *ALPIN*	
MACANDIE	(Bernera) Harris *MACLEOD*	B3
MACANDREW	*ROSS*; Inverness, *MACINTOSH*	G3, G4
MACANGUS ⎤ MACANISH ⎦	Argyll, Galloway, *MACINNES* Atholl, *MACGREGOR*	D5 F6
MACARA, MACAREE	Perthshire, *MACGREGOR*	F6
MACARA, MACARRA	Wester Ross, *MACRAE*	E4
MACARTHUR	Clan *MACARTHUR*	F6
	Skye, *MACDONALD*	C3
MACARTNEY	See MACCARTNEY	
MACASKIE	Galloway, from MAGASKILL	
MACASKILL	*MACLEOD* of Lewis	C4
MACASLAN, MACASLIN	*BUCHANAN*	F6
MACAULAY	*MACAULAY*; Clan *ALPIN*	F7
MACAULLY	*MACLEOD* of Lewis	B2
MACAUSELAN, MACAUSLAN, MACAUSLAND, MACAUSLANE	*BUCHANAN*	F6
MACAWEENEY	Same as MACWHINNIE	
MACAY	*SHAW*	H4
MACBAIN	*MACKAY*; *MACBEAN*	F2, I4
MACBAXTER	*MACMILLAN*	D7
MACBAY, MACBEY	*MACLEAN* of Duart	D6
MACBEAN	*MACBEAN*	I4
MACBEATH	Same as *MACBETH*	
MACBEOLAIN	*MACKENZIE*	F3
MACBETH ⎤ MACBHEATH ⎦	*MACBETH*; *MACBEAN* *MACDONALD*; *MACLEAN*	I3, I4 C3–D7, D6
MACBIRNIE	Galloway 15th c.; *MATHESON*	E4
MACBLAIN	Dumfries 12th c., Wigtownshire etc. 15th c.	
MACBRAIR	Dumfriesshire 15th c.	
MACBRAYNE	*MACNAUGHTON*; *MACDONALD*	E6, C7
MACBRIDE	Moray, Bute 14th c.; *MACDONALD*	D7
MACBRIEVE	*MORRISON*	C2
MACBRYDE	See MACBRIDE	
MACBURIE	*MACDONALD* of Clanranald	D5
MACBURNIE	Same as MACBIRNIE	
MACCAA	Galloway, from *MACKAY*	
MACCABE	Arran, *MACLEOD* of Lewis	C4
MACCAFFER	Islay, *MACDONALD*	C7
MACCAFFIE	From MACGUFFIE	
MACCAIG	Galloway 15th c.; *MACLEOD* of Harris; *FARQUHARSON*	C4, I5
MACCAINSH	From MACANGUS	
MACCAIRN	'MacCiaran', see MACKERRON	
MACCAIRTER	Same as *MACARTHUR*	
MACCAISH	See MACCASH	
MACCALL	Nithsdale, Bute 15th c.; *MACAULAY*	F7
MACCALLUM	*MACLEOD* of Lewis, to *MALCOLM*	D4, D7
MACCALMAN	MACCOLMAN, *BUCHANAN*	F6

SURNAME	CLAN OR DISTRICT SOURCE	KEY TO MAP
MACCALMONT	Ayr 16th c., from MACCOLMAN	
MACCAMBRIDGE	'MacAmbrose', *MACDONALD*	D7
MACCAMIE	FULLARTON, to Bute *STUART*	E7
MACCAMMOND	Galloway 17th c., from MACCOLMAN	
MACCANCE	From MACANGUS	
MACCANDLISH	Galloway 17th c.	
MACCANNELL	Islay etc. from *MACDONALD*	D7
MACCANSH	From MACANGUS	
MACCARDNEY	Same as MACHARDIE	
MACCARRON	'MacClaren', see MACKERRON	
MACCARTAIR, MACCARTER	Same as *MACARTHUR*	
MACCARTNEY	Galloway 16th c.; and MACHARDIE	
MACCASH	Perthshire, from MACTAVISH	
MACCASKIE	Galloway, from MACCASKILL	
MACCASKILL	*MACLEOD* of Lewis	C4
MACCASLAND	*BUCHANAN*	F6
MACCATHIE	Galloway 15th c.; *MACFIE*	C6
MACCAULEY	*MACAULAY*	F7, B2
MACCAUSE	Perthshire, Ayrshire 15th c.; MACTAVISH	
MACCAW	From *MACKAY*; Bute, to *STUART*	E7
MACCAY	See *MACKAY*	
MACCHEYNE	Galloway and Cowall 17th c.	
MACCHLERY	*CLAN CHATTAN: CAMERON*;	F5
	MACINTOSH; *MACPHERSON*	G4
MACCHRUITER	Carrick 14th c.; *BUCHANAN*	F6
MACCLAIR	From MACCHLERY	
MACCLANE	From *MACLEAN*	D6
MACCLARENCE	*MACLAREN*	G6
MACCLAY	From MACLEAY	
MACCLEAN	Ayrshire, *MACLEAN*	D6
MACCLEARY	From MACCHLERY	
MACCLEAY	*STEWART* of Appin	E5
MACCLEISH	See MACLEISH	
MACCLELLAND	From MACLELLAN	
MACCLEMENT	*LAMONT*	E7
MACCLINTOCK	See MACLINTOCK	
MACCLORY	Galloway 17th c.	
MACCLOY	See MACLOY	
MACCLUNG	Galloway 17th c.	
MACCLURE	Galloway 16th c.; Harris *MACLEOD*	C4
MACCLUSKIE	Kintyre etc.; *MACDONALD*	D7
MACCLYMONT	Ayrshire 17th c.; *LAMONT*	E7
MACCODRUM	North Uist, *MACDONALD*	A3
MACCOLL	*MACDONALD* to Appin *STEWART*	E5
MACCOLM	Same as MACCOMBE	
MACCOLMAN	Ayrshire 12th c.; *BUCHANAN*	F6
MACCOMAS	Same as MACOMISH	
MACCOMB, MACCOMBIE, MACCOMIE	Clan *MACTHOMAS*	I5
MACCOMBE	Galloway 16th c., Appin *STEWART*;	E5
	MACTHOMAS	
MACCOMBICH ⎫	*STEWART* of Appin	E5
MACCOMBIE ⎬	Angus, *MACTHOMAS*;	I5, G4
MACCOMIE ⎭	*MACINTOSH*	

SURNAME	CLAN OR DISTRICT SOURCE	KEY TO MAP
MACCONACHER	*MACDOUGALL*	E6
MACCONACHIE	Atholl, Bute, *ROBERTSON*	G5
	Argyll *CAMPBELL*; *MACGREGOR*	E5, F6
MACCONCHER	Lorne, *MACDOUGALL*	E6
MACCONCHIE	*MACFARLANE*	F6
MACCONDACH	See MACCONACHIE; *MACINTOSH*	G4
MACCONDOCHIE	*MACFARLANE*; *MACGREGOR*	F6
MACCONDY	MACCONACHIE, *MACGREGOR*	F6
MACCONICH	*ROBERTSON*	G5
MACCONNACH	*MACKENZIE*; *ROBERTSON*	F3, G5
MACCONNAL	See MACCONNELL	
MACCONNECHY	See MACCONACHIE	
MACCONNELL	S.W. Scotland, from *MACDONALD*	D7
MACCONOCHIE	See MACCONACHIE	
MACCOISH	*MACFIE*, to *MACDONALD*	C6, A3
MACCOOK	Kintyre etc., *MACDONALD*	D7
MACCORKILL	*GUNN*; Argyll, Lewis *MACLEOD*	H2, C4
MACCORKINDALE	See MACCORQUODALE	
MACCORKLE	See MACCORKILL	
MACCORMACK	Galloway 17th c.; *BUCHANAN*	F6
MACCORMICK	MACLAINE of Lochbuie	D6
MACCORQUODALE	Argyll 15th c.; *MACLEOD* of Lewis	C4
MACCORRY	*MACQUARRIE*	C5
MACCOSH	Ayrshire 16th c.	
MACCOSHAM	*MACINTYRE*; Skye, *MACDONALD*	E6, C4
MACCOUL	From *MACDOUGALL*	E9, E6
MACCOURT	Wigtownshire 15th c., Carrick 16th c.	
MACCOWAN	*MACDONNELL* of Glengarry, to	E4, F6
	MACDOUGALL; and from *COLQUHOUN*	
MACCOWATT	From MACWATT, *FORBES*	J4
MACCOWELL	From MACDOWELL	
MACCOYLE	Perthshire, from *MACDOUGALL*	E6
MACCRA, MACCRACH	Ayrshire etc. 17th c.; *MACRAE*	E4
MACCRACKEN	Galloway 16th c.; *MACNAUGHTON*	E6
MACCRAE, MACCREA	See MACCRA	
MACCRAIN, MACCRAN	Jura, Islay, *MACDONALD*	D–C7
MACCRAITH	See MACRAITH	
MACCRAW, MACCRAY	From *MACRAE*	E4
MACCREADIE	Galloway 17th c.	
MACCREATH	From *MACRAE*	E4
MACCREE, MACCRIE	Ayrshire 16th c.; *MACRAE*	E4
MACCRIMMON	Skye, *MACLEOD* of Harris	C4
MACCRINDLE	Galloway 15th c.; *MACDONALD* of Clanranald	D5
MACCRIRIE	Dumfriesshire 15th c.; *MACDONALD*	D7
MACCRONE	Galloway etc. 16th c.	
MACCRORIE	See MACRORIE	
MACCHROSTIE	Perthshire 16th c.	
MACCROUTHER	Same as MACGREWAR	
MACCROW, MACCROY	From *MACRAE*	E4
MACCRUITER	*MACGREGOR*	F6
MACCRUM	Benderloch, *MACDONALD*	D7
MACCUAIG	Islay, *MACDONALD*; *MACLEOD* of Harris,	C7, B3,
	FARQUHARSON	I5
MACCUBBIN,	MACGIBBON, Dumfriesshire etc. 14th c.;	F6
MACCUBBING	*BUCHANAN*	
MACCUBIE	MACGIBBON, Jedburgh 17th c.; *BUCHANAN*	F6

SURNAME	CLAN OR DISTRICT SOURCE	KEY TO MAP
MACCUISH	*MACFIE* to *MACDONALD*	C6, A3
MACCUITHEIN	Skye 17th c.; *MACDONALD*	C3
MACCULLAGH	See MACCULLOCH	
MACCULLIE	MACCULLOCH; Banffshire, *GUNN*	
MACCULLOCH	Galloway, Stewartry 11th c.; Argyll, E. Ross, from MacCullich	
MACCUNE, MACCUNN	Galloway 14th c.; from MACEWAN	
MACCURDY	Same as MACKIRDY	
MACCURE	From MACIVER	
MACCURRACH, MACCURRIE	From MACVURRICH	
MACCUTCHEN, MACCUTCHEON	*MACDONALD*	D4
MACDADE, MACDAID	Same as *DAVIDSON*	G4
MACDAIRMID	*CAMPBELL*	E6, G6
MACDANIELL	From *MACDONALD*	A3–D7
MACDAVID	*DAVIDSON*	G4
MACDERMID	*CAMPBELL*	E6, G6
MACDERMONT	*CAMPBELL*, Galloway	
MACDIARMID	*CAMPBELL*	E6, G6
MACDILL	Ayrshire 16th c.; *MACDOUGALL*	E6
MACDONACHIE	Same as MACCONNACHIE	
MACDONALD	Clan *MACDONALD* of the Isles	A3–D7
	MACDONALD of Clanranald	D5, C5, A4
	of Ardnamurchan; of Glencoe	D5, E5
MACDONELL	Clan *MACDONELL* of Glengarry;	F4–E3
	Clan *MACDONELL* of Keppoch	F5
MACDONLEAVY	Same as MACCLEAY	
MACDOOL, MACDOUL, MACDOUALL	Galloway, *MACDOUGALL*	E9
MACDOUGAL, MACDOUGALL	Clan *MACDOUGALL*	E9, E6
	also *MACGREGOR*	F6
MACDOWALL, MACDOWELL	Galloway, *MACDOUGALL*	E9
MACDRAIN	Kintyre, *MACDONALD*	D7
MACDUFF	Clan *MACDUFF*; Clan *ALPIN*	I6, J3
MACDUFFIE	*MACFIE*	C6
MACDUGALD	*MACDOUGALL*	E6
MACEACHAN, MACEACHEN	Carrick, Wigtown 13th c.; *MACDONALD* of Clanranald	D5, A4
MACEACHERN	Kintyre, *MACDONALD*	D7
MACEACHIN	See MACEACHAN	
MACEACHRAN	Same as MACEACHERN	
MACEARACHER	Same as MACERRACHER	
MACEDDIE	Inverness, *MUNRO*	G3
MACELEARY	Galloway, from MACCHLERY	
MACELFRISH	*MACDONALD*	A3
MACELHERAN	'MacCiaran' see MACKERRON	
MACELLAR	MACKELLAR, *CAMPBELL* of Argyll	E6
MACELVIE	MACKELVIE, *CAMPBELL* of Argyll	E6
MACERCHAR, MACERRACHER	Argyll, *LAMONT*; *MACFARLANE* Perthshire; *FARQUHARSON*	E7, F6 I5
MACEUR, MACEVER	Galloway, from MACIVER	
MACEWAN, MACEWEN	Cowal, Galloway, *MACLACHLAN*	E6
	Lorne, Perthshire, *MACDOUGALL*	E6
MACEWING	Galloway, *MACLACHLAN*	E6

SURNAME	CLAN OR DISTRICT SOURCE	KEY TO MAP
MACFADDEN	See MACFADYEN	
MACFADYEN, MACFADZEAN	Mull, *MACLAINE* of Lochbuie; to Galloway etc. 15th c.	D6
MACFAIL, MACFALL	From MACPHAIL, *MACINTOSH*	G4
MACFAIT, MACFADE	See MACFEAT	
MACFARLAN, MACFARLANE	Clan *MACFARLANE*	F6
MACFARQUHAR	Same as MACERCHAR	
MACFATER	See MACPHATER	
MACFAULD	From MACPHAIL	
MACFAYDEN	From MACFADYEN	
MACFEAT, MACFEAD	*MACLAREN*	G6
MACFEE	Same as *MACFIE*	C6
MACFERGUS	Lennox 16th c.; *FERGUSON*	I5
MACFIE	*MACFIE*; Clan *ALPIN*	C6
MACFETRIDGE	*MACLEAN*, to Ayrshire 16th c.	B5
MACGAA	Galloway, from MACKAY	
MACGACHAN	From MACEACHAN	
MACGAIR	*GAYRE*	
MACGARROW	Perthshire 16th c; *STEWART*	H5
MACGARVIE	Wigtownshire 15th c.	
MACGAW	Galloway, from *MACKAY*	
MACGEACH	*MACGREGOR*	F6
MACGEACHAN	From MACEACHAN	
MACGEACHY, MACGECHIE	*MACDONALD*	D7
MACGEE	See MACGHEE	
MACGEOCH	Wigtownshire 15th c.; *MACFARLANE*	F6
MACGEORGE	Galloway etc. 16th c.; from DEWAR	
MACGHEE, MACGHIE	Dumfries etc. 13th c.; *MACKAY*	
MACGIBBON	*BUCHANAN*; *CAMPBELL*	F6, E6
	GRAHAM of Menteith	G6
MACGILCHRIST	*MACLACHLAN*; *OGILVIE*	E6, J5
MACGILL	Galloway 13th c.; *MACDONALD*	D7
MACGILLECHALLUM	*MACLEOD* of Raasay	D4
MACGILLEDOW	*LAMONT*	E7
MACGILLERY	*CAMERON*	F5
MACGILLIES	Perthshire 12th c.; *MACPHERSON*	G4
MACGILLAVANTIC	*MACDONNELL* of Keppoch	F5
MACGILLIVRAY	Clan *MACGILLIVRAY*; Clan *CHATTAN*	G4
	MACLAINE of Lochbuie	D6—D5
MACGILLONIE	*CAMERON*	F5
MACGILP	From MACKILLOP	
MACGILROY	*GRANT*; *MACGILLIVRAY*	F4, G6
MACGILVERNOCK	Argyll, *GRAHAM* of Menteith	G6
MACGILVRA, MACGILVRAY	See *MACGILLIVRAY*	
MACGIRR	Galloway, Stewartry 17th c.	
MACGLASHAN, MACGLASHEN	Clan *CHATTAN: MACINTOSH*	G4
	Atholl *STEWART*, to *ROBERTSON*	G5
MACGLASHRICH	MACIVER, *CAMPBELL*	E6—G6
	MACDONNELL of Keppoch	F5
MACGORRIE, MACGORRY	*MACDONALD*	D7—C3
	Cowal, *LAMONT*; *MACQUARRIE*	E7, C5
MACGOUGAN	Kintyre, *MACNEILL* of Gigha	D7
MACGOUN, MACGOW	See MACGOWAN	

SURNAME	CLAN OR DISTRICT SOURCE	KEY TO MAP
MACGOWAN,	*MACDONALD*; *MACPHERSON*	C3−D7, G4
MACGOWN	Nithsdale 14th c.	
MACGRAIL	From *MACNEIL*	A4, D7
MACGRAIN	Galloway, from MACCRAIN	
MACGRATH,	From *MACRAE*	E4
MACGRAW		
MACGREGOR	Clan *MACGREGOR*; Clan *ALPIN*	F6, E6
MACGREUSICH	*BUCHANAN*; *MACFARLANE*	F6
MACGREWAR	*DRUMMOND*; *MACGREGOR*	H6, F6
	Beauly Firth, *FRASER*	F4
MACGRIGOR	*MACGREGOR*	F6
MACGRIME	*GRAHAM* of Menteith	G6
MACGRORY	*MACLAREN*	G6
MACGROUTHER,	Same as MACGREWAR	
MACGRUDER,		
MACGRUER,		
MACGRUTHER		
MACGRUMEN	*MACGREGOR*	F6
MACGUARIE	*MACQUARRIE*	C5
MACGUBBIN	From MACGIBBON	
MACGUFFIE	From MACGUFFOCK: also *MACFIE*	C6
MACGUFFOCK	Galloway 13th c., Aberdeen 14th c.; *DOUGLAS*	H8, J5
MACGUGAN,	Kintyre, *MACNEILL* of Gigha	D7
MACGUIGAN		
MACGUIRE	Ayrshire, from *MACQUARRIE*	C5
MACGURK	Lennox, *MACFARLANE*	F6
MACHAFFIE	From MACGUFFIE	
MACHALE	From *MACDOUGALL*	E9, E6
MACHARDY	Deeside; *FARQUHARSON*	I5
MACHARDIE	Donside; Clan *CHATTAN*; *MACINTOSH*	G4
MACHARG	Galloway 15th c.	
MACHAROLD	*MACLEOD* of Harris	C4
MACHAY	Dumfriesshire 14th c.; *SHAW*	H4
MACKHENDRIE,	N. Argyll; *MACDONALD* of Glencoe	F5
MACHENDRY,	Bute, S. Argyll; *MACNAUGHTON*	E6
MACHENRY		
MACHOWELL	From *MACDOUGALL*	E9, E6
MACHRAY	Aberdeenshire, from *MACRAE*	E4
MACHUGH,	*MACDONALD*	D4
MACHUTCHEN,		
MACHUTCHEON		
MACIAN	*MACDONALD* of Ardnamurchan	D5
	MACDONALD of Glencoe	F5
	Caithness, *GUNN*	H2
	also *MACGREGOR*	F6
MACILDOWIE	Duart *MACLEAN*; *CAMERON*	D6, F5
	LAMONT; *MACGREGOR*	E7, F6
MACILDUFF	Dumfries 15th c.; MACILDUY	
MACILDUY	*MACGREGOR*; *MACLEAN*	F6, D6
MACILLRICK	Ayrshire, MACILRIACH	
MACILREACH	See MACILRIACH	
MACILREVIE	Islay, Galloway, MACILRIACH	
MACILRIACH	N. Skye, S.W. Scotland, *MACDONALD*	C3
	Moray, N.E. Scotland, *FRASER*	F4
MACILROY	*GRANT* of Glenmoriston	F4
	Dumfriesshire 14th c.; *MACGILLIVRAY*	G4

SURNAME	CLAN OR DISTRICT SOURCE	KEY TO MAP
MACILVAIN, MACILVEEN	Galloway 14th c.; *MACBEAN*	I4
MACILVORA	*MACGILLIVRAY*; *MACLEAN*	D6
MACILVRAE	*MACGILLIVRAY*	D5, G4
MACILVRIDE	Perthshire 15th c.; *MACDONALD*	C3
MACILWHOM	From 'MacIlquham', *LAMONT*	E7
MACILWRAITH, MACILWRICK	S.W. Scotland, from MACILRIACH	
MACIMMEY	From MACSIMON, *FRASER*	F4—G4
MACINALLY	*MACFARLANE*; *BUCHANAN*	F6
MACINDEOR	Argyll, *BUCHANAN*; Islay, *MACARTHUR*; *MENZIES*	F6, G5
MACINDOE	*BUCHANAN*	F6
MACINNES	Clan *MACINNES*	D5
	Perthshire, *MACGREGOR*	F6
MACINNON	Skye, *MACKINNON*	D4
MACINROY	*ROBERTSON*	G5
MACINSTALKER	*MACFARLANE*; *MACGREGOR*	F6
MACINTOSH	Clan *MACINTOSH*; Clan *CHATTAN*	G4, H5, C2
MACINTYRE	Clan *MACINTYRE*	E6
MACISAAC	*MACDONALD* of Clanranald	D5, A4
	CAMPBELL of Argyll	E6
MACIVER, MACIVOR	Argyll, *CAMPBELL*	E6
	Ross and Lewis, *MACKENZIE*	F3
	Perthshire, *ROBERTSON*	H5
MACJAMES	*GUNN*; *MACFARLANE*; *ROBERTSON*	H2, F6, H5
MACK	Berwickshire 15th c.; *HOME*	K7
MACKAIL	From MACCALL, *MACAULAY*	F7
	From MACPHAIL, *CAMERON*	F5
MACKAIN, MACKANE	*MACDONALD* of Ardnamurchan	D5
MACKAMES	'MacJames', *GUNN*	H2
MACKASKILL	Skye, *MACLEOD* of Lewis	C4
MACKAY	Clan *MACKAY*	F2
	Argyll, Galloway, to *MACDONALD*	D7
MACKAY	Inverness-shire, *DAVIDSON*	G4
MACKEACHAN	From MACEACHAN	
MACKEACHIE	*MACDONALD*	D7
MACKEAMISH	'MacJames', *GUNN*	H2
MACKEAN, MACKEAND	From MACIAN	
MACKECHNIE	See MACEACHAN	
MACKEDDIE	From MACADIE	
MACKEE	Bute, Wigtown 16th c.; from *MACKAY*	
MACKEGGIE	See EGGIE; *MACINTOSH*	G4
MACKEITH	Perthshire, Argyll; *MACPHERSON*	G4
MACKEITHAN	From MACCUITHEIN, Skye 17th c.	
MACKELL	From MACKAIL	
MACKELLAIG	From MACKELLOCH	
MACKELLAR	*CAMPBELL* of Argyll	E6
MACKELLY, MACKELLOCH	Galloway 12th c., Perthshire etc. 14th c.; *MACDONALD*	A4—D7
MACKELVIE	Galloway 13th c.; *CAMPBELL*	E6
MACKENDRICK	MACHENRY; *MACNAUGHTON*	E6
MACKENNA, MACKENNEY	Wigtownshire 15th c., Bute 17th c.; from *MACKENZIE*	D3
MACKENZIE	Clan *MACKENZIE*	F3, D3
MACKEOCHAN	See MACEACHAN	

SURNAME	CLAN OR DISTRICT SOURCE	KEY TO MAP
MACKEON, MACKEOWN	See MACCUNE	
MACKERCHAR	See MACERCHAR	
MACKERLICH, MACKERLIE	Carrick 13th c.; Argyll, *CAMPBELL*; Ross, *MACKENZIE*	E6, F3
MACKERRACHER	From MACERRACHER	
MACKERRAS	Kintyre 16th c.; from MACFERGUS	
MACKERRELL	Ayrshire 13th c., Galloway 14th c.	
MACKERRON, MACKIARRAN	S.W. Scotland 12th c.; *MACDONALD* Bute, STUART; Moray, *GRANT*	D7 E7, H4
MACKERSEY	From MACKERRAS	
MACKESSACK, MACKESSICK	From MACISAAC; Moray 16th c.; *CAMPBELL* of Argyll	E6
MACKESTER	Kenmore 17th c.; *HAY*	I6
MACKEWAN, MACKEWN	See MACCUNE	
MACKEY	See MACKEE	
MACKICHAN	*MACDONALD* of Clanranald	D5, A4
	MACDOUGALL	E6
MACKIE (Mackie) (McKie)	Stirlingshire 16th c.; *MACKAY* See MACKEE	F3
MACKIESON	Moray 14th c.; *MACINTOSH*	G4
MACKIGGAN	N. Uist 16th c.; *MACDONALD*	A3
MACKILL	Galloway 15th c.	
MACKILLICAN	*MACINTOSH*	G4
MACKILLOP	*MACDONALD* of Glencoe	E5
	MACDONALD of Keppoch	F5
MACKIM, MACKIMMIE	From MACSIMON; *FRASER*	F4—G4
MACKINDLAY, MACKINLAY, MACKINLEY	Perthshire etc., *MACFARLANE, BUCHANAN*; West coast, from MACDONLEAVY; Deeside, *FARQUHARSON*	F6 I5
MACKINNELL	Dumfriesshire, *MACDONALD*	D7
MACKINNEY	From MACKENNA	
MACKINNING	From *MACKINNON*	
MACKINNON	Clan *MACKINNON*; Clan *ALPIN*	D4, E7
MACKINSTRY	Galloway 16th c.	
MACKINTOSH	From *MACINTOSH*	
MACKINTYRE	From *MACINTYRE*	E6
MACKINVEN	Kintyre 17th c.; *MACKINNON*	E7
MACKIRDY	Bute 16th c.; *STUART*	E7
MACKISSOCK	See MACKESSACK	
MACKIVER	Renfrew, from MACIVER	
MACKNIGHT	Galloway 16th c., from MACNAUGHT	
MACKUEN, MACKUNE	See MACCUNE	
MACLACHLAN	Clan *MACLACHLAN*	E6
MACLAE	See MACLEAY	
MACLAGAN	*ROBERTSON*	H5
MACLAGHLAN	*MACLACHLAN*	E6
MACLAINE	Clan *MACLAINE* of Lochbuie	D6
MACLAIRISH	*MACDONALD*	A3, C3
MACLAMOND	*LAMONT*	E7
MACLARDY	From MACLAVERTY	
MACLAREN	Clan *MACLAREN*	G6
MACLARTY	From MACLAVERTY	

SURNAME	CLAN OR DISTRICT SOURCE	KEY TO MAP
MACLATCHIE	Ayrshire 16th c.	
MACLAUCHLAN, MACLAUGHLIN	Clan *MACLACHLAN*	E6
MACLAURIN	Same as *MACLAREN*	G6
MACLAVERTY	Galloway 14th c.; *MACDONALD*	D7
MACLAWS	From MACLEHOSE	
MACLAY, MACLEA	See MACLEAY	
MACLEAN	Clan *MACLEAN*	D6—B5, E5
MACLEAR, MACLEARY	From MACCHLERY	
MACLEAY	Ross 15th c.; Appin *STEWART*	E5
MACLEES, MACLEESH	Same as MACLEISH	
MACLEHOSE	*CAMPBELL*; Perthshire, *MACTHOMAS*	E6, I5
MACLEISH	Dumfriesshire 14th c.; from MACGILLIES	
MACLEISTER	Argyll etc., *MACGREGOR*	F5
MACLELLAN, MACLELLAND	'MacGilfillan', Galloway 13th c., Inverness 15th c., Perthshire, *MACNAB*	F6
MACLEMON	*LAMONT*	E7
MACLENNAN	Clan *MACLENNAN*	E4
MACLEOD	*MACLEOD* of Harris	B3, C4, E4
	MACLEOD of Lewis	C2—4, D3—4
MACLERGAIN	Islay, *MACLEAN*	D6
MACLERIE	From MACCHLERY	
MACLETCHIE	Ayrshire 13th c.	
MACLEVERTY	See MACLAVERTY	
MACLEW	Same as MACLEAY	
MACLEWIS	From MACLOUIS: also *MACLEOD*	C2—D4
MACLINDEN	From MACLINTOCK	
MACLINTOCK	*COLQUHOUN*; Lorne, *MACDOUGALL*	F6—E6
MACLISE, MACLISH	See MACLEISH, *MACPHERSON*	G4
MACLIVER	*MACGREGOR*; Islay, *CAMPBELL*	F6, E6
MACLORG, MACLURG	Ayrshire 13th c.	
MACLOUIS, MACLOY	Arran, FULLARTON; *STUART*	E7
MACLUCAS		
MACLUCKIE	Cowal, *LAMONT*	E7
MACLUGASH	N. Argyll, *MACDOUGALL*	E6
MACLUKE		
MACLULLICH	*MACDOUGALL*; *ROSS*; *MUNRO*	E6, G3
MACLUNG	Galloway 17th c.	
MACLURE	Galloway 16th c.; Harris *MACLEOD*	C4
MACLYMONT	Carrick 17th c.; *LAMONT*	E7
MACMAHON	*MATHESON*	E4
MACMAINS, MACMANUS	From 'MacMagnus', *COLQUHOUN*; *GUNN*	F6, H2
MACMARTIN	Galloway 12th c.; *CAMERON*	F5
MACMASTER	*MACINNES*; *BUCHANAN*	D5, F6
MACMATH	*MATHESON*; Dumfries, MACNAUGHT	
MACMAURICE	*BUCHANAN*	F6
MACMEEKEN, MACMEIKAN	See MACMICHAN	
MACMENZIES	Dumfriesshire etc. 14th c.; *MENZIES*	H5
MACMICHAEL	Appin and Galloway *STEWART*	E5, H8
	Aberdeenshire, see MACMICHIE	
MACMICHAN	Carrick and Galloway 12th c.	
MACMICHIE	*MACDONELL* of Keppoch	F5
MACMILLAN	Clan *MACMILLAN*	D7

SURNAME	CLAN OR DISTRICT SOURCE	KEY TO MAP
MACMIN, MACMINN	Galloway 15th c.; *MENZIES*	H5
MACMONIES	Dumfries 16th c.; *MENZIES*	H5
MACMORINE	Galloway, MACMORRAN	
MACMORRAN	Galloway 14th c.; Mull, *MACKINNON*	D4
MACMUNN	*LAMONT*, to Bute *STUART*	F6, E7
MACMURCHIE	N. Uist, Kintyre, *MACDONALD*	D7, A3
MACMURCHY	*BUCHANAN*; *MACKENZIE*	F6, E3
MACMURDO, MACMURDOCH	Kintyre to Dumfriesshire 16th c. *MACDONALD*; *MACPHERSON*	D7, G4
MACMURRAY	Galloway, from MACVURICH	
MACMURRICH	From MACVURICH	
MACMURTRIE	Ayrshire etc., from MACKIRDY	
MACNAB, MACNABB	*MACNAB*; Clan *ALPIN*	F6
MACNACHTAN, MACNAUGHTEN	Same as *MACNAUGHTON*	E6
MACNAIR	Argyll, *MACNAUGHTON*; Lennox, *MACFARLANE*; Perthshire, *MACNAB*	E6, F6
MACNAIRN	Dumfriesshire 14th c.; Appin *STEWART*	E5
MACNAMELL	From '*MACMILLAN*', to *MACDOUGALL*	D7, E6
MACNAUCHTON	Same as *MACNAUGHTON*	E6
MACNAUGHT	Dumfriesshire 13th c.; *MACNAUGHTON*	E6
MACNAUGHTAN, MACNAUGHTON	Clan *MACNAUGHTON*	E6
MACNAY	Same as MACNEE	F6
MACNAYER	Same as MACNAIR	
MACNEAL, MACNEALE	*MACNEIL*	A4, A5, D7
MACNEE, MACNEA	*MACGREGOR*	F6
MACNEICE	Same as MACNEISH	F6
MACNEIL ⎫	Clan *MACNEIL* of Barra	A4–A5
MACNEILL ⎭	Clan *MACNEILL* of Gigha	D7
MACNEILAGE	Lennox 15th c.; *MACNEIL*	D7
MACNEISH	*MACINNES*; Dumfriesshire 14th c.; Strathearn, *MACGREGOR*	F6
MACNELLY	Galloway 13th c.; *MACNEIL*	D7
MACNESS	Same as MACNEISH	
MACNEUR	Same as MACNUIR	
MACNEVIN	Same as MACNIVEN	
MACNEY	*MACGREGOR*	F6
MACNICOL MACNICOLL MACNICHOL	Sutherland and Skye, MACLEOD of Lewis; Glenorchy, *MACFIE* to *CAMPBELL*	E2, E6
MACNIDER	Ayrshire 15th c.; *MACFARLANE*	F6
MACNIE	*MACGREGOR*	F6
MACNIEL	Same as *MACNEIL*	A4, A5, D7
MACNEISH, MACNISH	See MACNEISH	
MACNIFF	Kirkcudbrightshire 17th c.	
MACNITER	See MACNIDER	
MACNIVEN	Argyll, *MACNAUGHTON*, to *CAMPBELL*	E6
	Spey, *MACINTOSH*; *CUMMING*	G4, G5
MACNOCAIRD	*MACGREGOR*; *CAMPBELL*	F6, E5
MACNUCATOR	*MACGREGOR*; Appin *STEWART*	F6, E5
MACNUIR, MACNUYER	Cowal: *MACNAUGHTON*, *BUCHANAN*	E6, F6
	Lennox: *MACFARLANE*	F6
MACOMIE	From *MACTHOMAS*, *MACINTOSH*	I5, H5
MACOMISH	*MACTHOMAS*; *GUNN*	I5, H2
MACONACHIE	See MACCONOCHIE	

SURNAME	CLAN OR DISTRICT SOURCE	KEY TO MAP
MACONIE	*CAMERON*	F5
MACORAN	*CAMPBELL* of Argyll	E6
MACO'SHANNAIG	Kintyre 16th c.; *MACDONALD*	D7
MACOSTRICH	From 'Macostric'; *CAMERON*	F5
MACOUAL, MACOUL	From *MACDOUGALL*	E9, E6
MACOUAT, MACOWAT	From MACWATT, *FORBES*	J4
MACOWAN, MACOWEN	See MACCOWAN	
MACPARLAND, MACPARLANE	From *MACFARLANE*	F6
MACPATRICK	*LAMONT*; *MACLAREN*	E7, G6
MACPETER	Ayrshire 17th c.; *MACGREGOR*	F6
MACPETRIE	*MACLAREN*; *MACGREGOR*	G6, F6
MACPHADDEN	From MACFADYEN, *MACLEAN*	D5
MACPHAIL	*CAMERON*; Clan *CHATTAN*	F5
	MACINTOSH; *MACKAY*	G4, F2
MACPHAIT	*MACLAREN*	G6
MACPHATER	Argyll, *MACLAREN*	G6
MACPHEDRAN ⎫	Loch Fyne, *MACAULAY*	F6
MACPHEDRON ⎭	Lochawe branch, to *CAMPBELL*	E6
MACPHEE	Same as *MACFIE*	C6
MACPHIEDRAN	Same as MACPHEDRAN	
MACPHERSON	Clan *MACPHERSON*; Clan *CHATTAN*	G4
MACPHIE	Same as *MACFIE*	C6
MACPHILIP	Same as *MACKILLOP*	
MACPHUN	MACMUNN to *MACARTHUR*	F6
MACQUAIRE	*MACQUARRIE*	C5
MACQUAKER	Galloway 17th c., from MACVICAR	
MACQUARIE, MACQUARRIE	*MACQUARRIE*, Clan *ALPIN*	C5
MACQUAT	Dumfries 16th c., from MACWATT	
MACQUATTIE	From MACWATTIE	
MACQUE, MACQUEY	Galloway 17th c., from *MACKAY*	
MACQUEEN	Clan *MACQUEEN*; Clan *CHATTAN*	C3
MACQUEENIE	Galloway 16th c., from *MACKENZIE*	F3
MACQUHIRR	Galloway 16th c., from *MACQUARRIE*	C5
MACOUIKCAN	Kintyre 16th c.; *MACDONALD*	D7
MACQUIRE	From *MACQUARRIE*	C5
MACQUISTAN, MACQUISTEN	Same as MACHUTCHEN	
MACQUOID	*MACKAY*	F2
MACRA, MACRACH	Ayrshire etc. 17th c.; *MACRAE*	E4
MACRAE	Clan *MACRAE*	E4
MACRAILD	*MACLEOD* of Harris	C4
MACRAITH	From *MACRAE*; *MACDONALD*	E4, D7
MACRANKIN	Ayrshire 16th c.; Coll, *MACLEAN*	D6
MACRATH	From *MACRAE*	E4
MACRAW, MACRAY	From *MACRAE*	
MACREARIE	Dumfriesshire 15th c.; *MACDONALD*	D7
MACRIE	See MACRA	
MACRIMMON	Skye, *MACLEOD* of Harris	C4
MACRITCHIE	Glenshee, *MACINTOSH*	H5
MACROB, MACROBB	Perthshire, *MACFARLANE*; *INNES*	F6, I3
	STEWART of Appin; *GUNN*	E5, G2
MACROBBIE	*ROBERTSON*; *DRUMMOND*	H5, H6
MACROBERT, MACROBERTS	*ROBERTSON*	H5

SURNAME	CLAN OR DISTRICT SOURCE	KEY TO MAP
MACROBIE	Same as MACROBBIE	
MACRONALD	*MACDONELL* of Keppoch	F5
MACRORIE, MACRORY, MACRURY	*MACDONALD*; *MACLAREN*	A3—D7, G6
MACRUER	MACGREWAR, *MACDONALD*	D7
MACRYRIE	*MACDONALD*	A3—D7
MACSHERRIE	Skye, Mull, *MACKINNON*	D4
MACSIMON	*FRASER*: *MACARTHUR*	F4, F6
MACSORLEY	*LAMONT*, to (Islay) *MACDONALD*, and to *CAMERON*	E7, C7, F5
MACSPORRAN	Argyll 12th c.; *MACDONALD* (also recognised in the 1970s by Lord Lyon as a clan in its own right)	A3—D7
MACSTEVEN	Ayrshire 16th c.	
MACSWAIN	*MACQUEEN*	C3
MACSWAN, MACSWEEN	*MACQUEEN*; *MACDONALD*	C3, D7
MACSYMON	See MACSIMON	
MACTAGGART	Dumfries 15th c. etc.; *ROSS*	G3
MACTAUSE	From MACTAVISH	
MACTAVISH	*CAMPBELL*; Strathglass, *FRASER* Perthshire, see *MACTHOMAS*	E6, F4
MACTEAR	See MACTIER	
MACTHOMAS	Perthshire, Angus 14th c., Clan *MACTHOMAS*; *MACINTOSH*; Clan *CHATTAN*	
MACTIER, MACTIRE	*ROSS*; Ayrshire, Galloway 16th c.; from *MACINTYRE*	G3, E6
MACTURK	Wigtownshire 16th c.	
MACULRIG	*CAMERON*	F5
MACURE	From MACIVER	
MACVAIL	From MACPHAIL	
MACVAIN, MACVANE	*MACKENZIE*	F3, D3
MACVANISH	From MACBAIN	
MACVARISH	*MACDONALD* of Clanranald	D5
MACVAY, MACVEAGH	*MACLEAN* of Duart	D6
MACVEAN	Same as *MACBEAN*	I4
MACVEE	From *MACFIE*	C6
MACVEY	*MACLEAN* of Duart	D6
MACVICAR	*MACNAUGHTON*, to *CAMPBELL*	E6
MACVIE	From *MACFIE*	C6
MACVINISH	*MACKENZIE*	F3, D3
MACVINNIE	From MACWHINNIE	
MACVITTIE	Galloway 16th c.	
MACVURIE	*MACDONALD* of Clanranald	D5
MACVURICH, MACVURRICH	Argyll, Arran, *MACDONALD* of Clanranald; Perthshire,. *MACPHERSON*	D5, G4
MACWALRICK	*KENNEDY*, to *CAMERON*	F8, F5
MACWALTER	Ayrshire 16th c.; *MACFARLANE*	F6
MACWATT	Bute etc. 15th c.; *FORBES*	J4
MACWATTIE	*BUCHANAN*; *FORBES*	F6, J4
MACWEENY	See MACWHINNIE	
MACWHAN	*MACDONALD*; *MACQUEEN*	D7, C3
MACWHANNELL	Ayr, Perth 16th c.; *MACDONALD*	D7
MACWHINNIE	Galloway 16th c.; from *MACKENZIE*	F3
MACWHIRR	Dumfries 16th c.; *MACQUARRIE*	C5
MACWHIRTER	From MACCHRUITER	

SURNAME	CLAN OR DISTRICT SOURCE	KEY TO MAP
MACWILLIAM	*MACLEOD* of Harris; *GUNN*	C4, H2
	MACFARLANE; *ROBERTSON*	F6, H5
	also *MACGREGOR*	F6
MAGREW	*MACGREGOR*	F6
MAIN, MAGNUS	Moray, Nairn, etc., *GUNN*	H2
	From 'Mayne', Perthshire 16th c.	
MAINLAND	Orkney, Shetland 16th c.	
MAIR, MAJOR	Perthshire etc. 13th c.	
MAITLAND	Lauderdale 12th c.	
MALCOLM, MALCOM	Clan *MALCOLM*	D7, D4
MALCOLMSON	Berwickshire 13th c.; *MACLEOD*	D4
MALLACE	Perth (Malles) to Angus 15th c.	
MALLISON	Aberdeen, Dundee 15th c.	
MALLOCH	Perth, Angus 15th c.; *MACGREGOR*	F6
MALLOY	See MILLOY	
MALTMAN	Aberdeenshire 16th c.	
MANDERSON	Merse (Manderston) 15th c.	
MANN, MANSON	'Magnus-son', *GUNN*	H2
MANUEL	Stirlingshire (Manuel) 13th c.	
MARCHBANKS	From MARJORIBANKS	
MARGACH	Moray 17th c.	
MARJORIBANKS	Renfrewshire 16th c.; *JOHNSTON*	I8
MARK	Roxburghshire 16th c.; *MACDONALD*	D7
MARQUIS	From MacMarquis; *MACDONALD*	D7
MARR	Fife, Aberdeenshire 13th c.; *GORDON*	I4
MARSHALL	Lothian etc. 12th c.; *KEITH*	K5
MARTIN	*CAMERON*; *MACDONALD*	F5, C3
MARTIN, MARTINE	E. Lothian, Angus 12th c.	
MARWICK	Orkney (W. Mainland) 17th c.	
MASON, MASSON	Berwick, Midlothian etc. 14th c.	
MASSEY, MASSIE	Aberdeenshire 17th c.; *MATHESON*	E4
MASTERS	Same as MACMASTER	
MASTERSON, MASTERTON	Fife (Dunfermline) 13th c.	
MATHER, MATHERS	Fife 13th c., Angus 15th c.	
MATHESON	Clan *MATHESON*	E4
	Angus etc. 14th c.; and from MACMATH	
MATHEWSON	See *MATHESON*	
MATHIE	Angus 15th c.; *MATHESON*	
MATHIESON	See *MATHESON*	
MATSON, MATTHEW	See *MATHESON*	
MAUCHLEN	Ayrshire (Mauchline) 15th c.	
MAULE	Midlothian 12th c., Angus etc. 13th c.	
MAVER, MAVOR	Speymouth 15th c.; *GORDON*	I4
MAXTON	Dryburgh 13th c., to Perthshire 14th c.	
MAXWELL	Clan *MAXWELL*	H8
MAY	Berwick 13th c., Fife 14th c.; and OMAY	
MEANIE, MEANEY	Aberdeenshire (Meanie) 17th c.	
MEANIES, MEANS	From *MENZIES*	H5, G5
MECHIE, MEKIE	From MICHIE	
MEECHAN, MEEHAN	From MACMICHAN	
MEEK, MEIK	Fife, Angus 15th c., Perthshire 16th c.	
MEEKISON	From MACMICHIE	
MEFFAN, MEFFET	See METHVEN; *MOFFAT*	
MEIKLE	Aberdeenshire, Moray 14th c.	
MEIKLEHAM	From 'MacIlquham', *LAMONT*	E7

| --- | --- | --- |
MEIKLEJOHN	Fife etc. 17th c.	
MEIKLEM	See MEIKLEHAM	
MEIN, MEINE	Roxburgh 14th c.; and from *MENZIES*	H5
MELDRUM	*FORBES*; *GORDON*	J4
MELLIS, MELLISH	Aberdeenshire 15th c. ('Malise')	
MELLON, MELLEN	Moray Firth, from MELVIN	
MELROSE	Roxburghshire 15th c.	
MELVILLE	Midlothian, Angus 12th c.	I7
MELVIN, MELVEN	Angus etc. 14th c., from MELVILLE	
MENELAWS	E. Ross and Lauder 15th c.	
MENGUES	From *MENZIES*	H5, G5
MENTEITH	*GRAHAM*; *STEWART*	G6, H7
MENTIPLAY	Caithness 17th c., from MONEYPENNY	
MENZIES	Clan *MENZIES*	H5, G6
MERCER	Tillicoultry, Perth etc. 13th c.	
MERCHANT	Fife and Angus 13th c.	
MERRILEES	W. Lothian 16th c.	
MESSENGER	Midlothian, Dumfries 17th c.	
MESSER	Stirlingshire 15th c., Aberdeen etc. 17th c.	
METHVEN, METHUEN	Perthshire (Methven) 13th c.	
MICHAEL	Angus 15th c.; Keppoch *MACDONNELL*	F5
MICHIE	Keppoch *MACDONNELL*, to *FORBES*	F5, J4
MICHIESON	From MACMICHIE	
MICKEL, MICKLE	Same as MEIKLE	
MIDDLEMASS, MIDDLEMIST, etc.	Kelso, to Peeblesshire 15th c.	
MIDDLETON	Laurencekirk 13th c.; *FORBES*	J4
MILES	Melrose etc. 16th c.	
MILL	Angus, Aberdeen 15th c.; *GORDON*	J4
MILLAR, MILLER	Moray 14th c., Glasgow etc. 15th c.; *MACFARLANE*	F6
MILLIGAN	Galloway 13th c., Perth 15th c.	
MILLIKEN	Same as MILLIGAN	
MILLOY	From MACLOY, *STUART* of Bute	E7
MILLS, MILN, MILNE, MILNES	Aberdeenshire 14th c.; *GORDON*	J4
MILROY	From MACILROY, *MACGILLIVRAY*	G4
MINN, MINNUS	Galloway, from *MENZIES*	H5
MINTO	Teviotdale (Minto) 17th c.	
MIRK	Glasgow 15th c., Kelso etc. 16th c.	
MITCHELHILL	Peeblesshire, to Selkirk 16th c.	
MITCHELL	From MACMICHAEL; Lanarkshire 15th c.	
MITCHELSON	Fife 14th c., and MACMICHAEL	
MOAR	Orkney 15th c.	
MOCHRIE	S.E. Stirlingshire 17th c.	
MOFFAT, MOFFETT	Annandale 13th c. (now recognised as a clan in its own right)	
MOIR	Aberdeenshire 14th c.; *GORDON*	K4
MOLLISON	Aberdeen 16th c.; from MALLISON	
MONACH	Perthshire, *MACFARLANE*	F6
MONCRIEFF	Strathearn, to Angus 13th c.	I6
MONCUR	Fife 13th c., Angus 14th c.	
MONRO, MONROE	Same as *MUNRO*	G3
MONTEATH, MONTEITH	Same as MENTEITH	
MONTGOMERIE, MONTGOMERY	Renfrewshire 12th c.	F7

SURNAME	CLAN OR DISTRICT SOURCE	KEY TO MAP
MONYPENNY	Fife 13th c., Stirlingshire 15th c.	
MOODIE, MOODY	Tweed 13th c., Angus 15th c.; *STEWART*	H5
MOORE	Same as MUIR	
MORAY	Same as *MURRAY*	G2, H6
MORE	From MOIR, also MUIR; *LESLIE*	J4
MORGAN	Aberdeenshire etc. 13th c.; *MACKAY*	F2
MORHAM, MORAM	E. Lothian 12th c., Angus etc. 13th c.	
MORISON	Clan *MORRISON*; Perthshire, *BUCHANAN*	C2, F6
MORREN, MORRIN	Dumfries etc., from MACMORRAN	
MORRIS, MORRICE	Ayrshire, Aberdeen etc. 16th c.; *GORDON*; Perthshire, *BUCHANAN*	J4, F6
MORRISON	Clan *MORRISON*; Perthshire, *BUCHANAN*	C2, F6
MORTIMER	Fife etc. 12th c.	
MORTON	Nithsdale 12th c., Fife 14th c.; *DOUGLAS*	H8
MOSS	Nithsdale 14th c., Tweed 16th c.	
MOSSMAN	Tweed 15th c., Edinburgh etc. 16th c.	
MOUAT, MOWATT	Angus 12th c., Cromarty 13th c.; *SUTHERLAND*	G2
MOULTRIE	Berwick 13th c., Edinburgh 14th c.	
MOUNSEY, MOUNSIE	Roxburghshire 13th c., Lochmaben 14th c.	
MOWBRAY	Fife, Lothian 12th c.	
MOYES	Angus 13th c., Lanarkshire 15th c.	
MUCKHART	Clackmannanshire 13th c., Aberdeen 16th c.	
MUDIE	See MOODIE	
MUIL, MUILL	Nairn 13th c., Aberdeen etc. 17th c.	
MUIR, MURE	Galloway, Ayrshire 13th c.; *GORDON*	J4
MUIRHEAD	Roxburghshire 14th c., Lanarkshire 15th c.	
MUNDELL, MUNDLE	Dumfriesshire, Wigtownshire 13th c.	
MUNGALL, MUNGLE	Falkirk, to Ayrshire etc. 13th c.	
MUNN	From MACMUNN	
MUNNOCH, MUNNOCK	Fife etc., from MONACH	
MUNRO, MUNROE	Clan *MUNRO*	G3
MUNSIE	See MOUNSIE	
MURCHIE, MURCHISON	From MACMURCHIE	
MURDOCH, MURDOCK	From MACMURCHIE, also MACMURDOCH	
MURDOSON	*MACDONALD*; *MACPHERSON*	D7, G4
MURIE	Gowrie (Murie) 17th c.	
MURISON	Fife, Angus, Aberdeenshire 15th c.	
MURPHY	Arran, Kintyre, *MACDONALD*	D7
MURRAY	*MURRAY*; *SUTHERLAND*	H6, G2
MURRIE	Perthshire, *MURRAY*	H6
MUSHET	Angus etc. 12th c.; *DRUMMOND*	H6
MUSTARD	Angus etc. 16th c.	
MUTCH	Stirlingshire 16th c.	
MUTRIE	From MOULTRIE	
MYLES	See MILES	
MYLNE	See MILNE	
NAIRN, NAIRNE	Nairn etc. 14th c.; *MACINTOSH*	G4
NAISMITH	Angus 15th c., Lanarkshire etc. 16th c.	
NAPIER, NAPPER	Lennox 13th c.; *MACFARLANE*; *SCOTT*	F6, I8
NASMYTH, NAYSMITH	See NAISMITH	
NEAL, NEALE	*MACNEIL*	A4, D7
NEAVES	From BALNEAVES, *MURRAY*	G5
NEIL, NEILL	*MACNEIL*	A4, D7
NEILLANDS	From NEWLANDS	

SURNAME	CLAN OR DISTRICT SOURCE	KEY TO MAP
NEILSON	*MACKAY*, and to *GUNN*	F2, H2
	Ayrshire 13th c.; *STUART* of Bute	E7
	From *MACNEIL*	A4, D7
NEISH	From MACNEISH, *MACGREGOR*	F6
NELSON	Same as NEILSON; *MACGREGOR*	F6
NESBET, NESBITT	Same as NISBET	
NESS	Fife and Renfrewshire 12th c.	
NEVILLE	Perth 13th c.	
NEVIN, NEVISON	See NIVEN, NIVISON	
NEWBIGGING	Lanarkshire 13th c., etc.	
NEWLANDS	Dumfriesshire, W. Lothian 15th c.	
NEWTON	Midlothian 13th c., etc.	
NICE	See NISH	
NICOL, NICHOL ⎫ NICOLL, NICHOLL ⎬	Roxburghshire, Angus 12th c.; also from MACNICOL	
NICHOLS, NICOLS ⎫ NICOLSON NICHOLSON ⎬	From NICHOLAS; Glasgow, Aberdeen etc. 15th c. From MACNICOL, *MACLEOD* of Lewis	E2, C4
NIEL, NIELSON	See NEIL, NEILSON	
NIMMO	W. Lothian 15th c., Glasgow 16th c.	
NISBET, NISBETT	Berwickshire 12th c.; *HOME*	K7
NISH, NICE	From MACNEISH; Fife, from NESS	
NIVEN, NIVISON	Lanarkshire 13th c., Ayrshire 16th c.; and from MACNIVEN	
NIXON	Liddesdale 14th c.; *ARMSTRONG*	J8
NOBLE	E. Lothian 12th c.; *MACINTOSH*	G4
NOON	Aberdeen 16th c.	
NORIE, NORRIE	Orkney etc.; Lewis *MACLEOD*	C2
NORMAN, NORMAND	Aberdeen, Tweed (Normanville) 12th c.	B3
	From 'Tormod'; Harris *MACLEOD*	
NORRIS	Berwickshire 12th c.	
NORVAL, NORWELL	From 'Normanville': see NORMAN	
NOTMAN	E. Lothian 16th c.	
NUCATOR	Angus 16th c., from MACNUCATOR	
OAG, OAKE	Same as OGG	
OCHILTREE	W. Lothian 14th c.; *CAMPBELL*	E6
OFFICER	Kincardineshire etc. 13th c.	
OGG	Aberdeenshire 15th c.	
OGILBY	Same as *OGILVIE*	
OGILVIE, OGILVY	Clan *OGILVIE*	J5, J3
OGSTON, OGSTOUN	Elgin 13th c.	
OLIPHANT	Roxburghshire, OLIVER; *SUTHERLAND*	J8, G2
OLIVER	Roxburghshire 12th c.; *FRASER*	J8, F4
OLLASON	Shetland 16th c.	
OMAN, OMAND	Orkney, Shetland 16th c.	
OMAY, O'MAY	Kintyre 16th c.; *MACDONALD*	D7
ORAM, OREM	Aberdeen 15th c.	
ORKNEY	Angus etc. 15th c.	
ORMISTON	Roxburghshire, E. Lothian 12th c.	
ORR	S.W. Renfrewshire 13th c.; *CAMPBELL* of Argyll; *MACGREGOR*	F6
ORROCK, ORRICK	Fife (Burntisland) 13th c.	
OSBORN, OSBORNE	Ayrshire etc. 16th c.	
OSLER, OSTLERE	Moray 15th c.	

SURNAME	CLAN OR DISTRICT SOURCE	KEY TO MAP
OSWALD	Ayrshire, Fife, Orkney 17th c.	
OTTER	Berwick 13th c., Fife 15th c.	
OVENS	E. Lothian 17th c.	
PADON	Same as PATON	
PAGAN, PAIN	Renfrewshire 13th c.	
PAGE	Aberdeenshire, Angus 14th c.	
PAINTER, PANTER	Angus 14th c.	
PAIRMAN	E. Teviotdale 16th c.	
PAISLEY	Renfrewshire 12th c.	
PALMER	Tweedside, Glasgow etc. 13th c.	
PANTON	Lanarkshire 13th c., Aberdeenshire 15th c.	
PAPE	Same as POPE	
PAPLAY	Orkney 14th c.	
PARIS	Ayrshire etc. 13th c.	
PARK, PARKE	Renfrew (Erskine), to Berwickshire 13th c.; S. Uist, *MACDONALD* of Clanranald	A4
PARKER	Perthshire 13th c., Dundee 14th c.	
PARLAN, PARLANE	From *MACFARLANE*	
PATE	Fife 16th c., Lanarkshire 17th c.	
PATERSON	From MACPHEDRAN: also MACPATRICK	
PATTERSON	Aberdeenshire, *FARQUHARSON*	I5
PATON	*MACDONALD*; Lochbuie *MACLAINE*	D7, D6
PATRICK	Ayrshire 15th c.; and from MACPATRICK	
PATTEN, PATTON ⎫	See PATON	
PATTIE, PATTISON ⎭	Fife 16th c., Paisley etc. 16th c.	
PATTINSON	Edinburgh, Aberdeen 15th c., Dumfries 16th c.	
PATTULLO	Fife, Perth 14th c.; *MACGREGOR*	F6
PAUL	See MACPHAIL	
PAULIN, PAULINE	W. Lothian, Angus 14th c.	
PAXTON	E. Berwickshire (Paxton) 13th c.	
PEACE	Orkney 15th c.	
PEACOCK	Dumfriesshire 13th c.	
PEARSON	Berwickshire 15th c.; *MACPHERSON*	G4
PEAT	Aberdeen 15th c., from PETER	
PEATTIE, PEDDIE	Fife and Angus 15th c.	
PEDEN	Ayrshire 17th c., from PATON	
PEEBLES	Tweeddale, also Angus 14th c.	
PENDER	Lanarkshire 16th c.	
PENDREICH	Stirlingshire, PITTENDREIGH	
PENMAN	Tweedside 17th c.	
PENNEY, PENNY	Moray and Perthshire 14th c.	
PENNYCOOK, etc.	Midlothian (Penicuik) 13th c.	
PENTLAND	Midlothian 13th c.	
PERRY	Angus 15th c., Aberdeen 17th c.	
PETER	Aberdeen 14th c.; *MACGREGOR*	F6
PETERKIN	Aberdeen 15th c.; *MACGREGOR*	F6
PETERS, PETERSON	*MACLAREN*; *MACGREGOR*	G6, F6
PETRIE	*MACLAREN*; *MACGREGOR*	G6, F6
PETTIE, PETTITT	Lanarkshire 13th c., Ayr etc. 14th c.	
PETTIGREW	Lanarkshire 13th c.	
PHILP, PHILLIP ⎫ PHILIPSON PHILLIPS ⎬ PHILP, PHILPOT ⎭	Berwick and Lanarkshire 13th c., Aberdeen and Fife 15th c.; also from MACKILLOP	
PHIMISTER	Moray 15th c.	

SURNAME	CLAN OR DISTRICT SOURCE	KEY TO MAP
PHIN	Fife 16th c., Banffshire 16th c.	
PICKEN	Ayrshire, Edinburgh 17th c.	
PIGGOT, PIGOTT	Berwickshire, Aberdeenshire 14th c.	
PILLAN, PILLANS	Lanarkshire (Carstairs) 16th c.	
PINKERTON	E. Lothian 13th c., to *CAMPBELL* 16th c.	E6
PIPER, PYPER	Perthshire 16th c.; *MURRAY*	H6, G2
PIRIE, PIRRIE	Aberdeenshire, Renfrewshire 15th c.	
PITCAIRN	Fife (Pitcairn) 13th c.	
PITKETHLY, etc.	E. Strathearn (Pitcaithly) 13th c.	
PITTENDREIGH	Moray 13th c., Wigtown 14th c. etc.	
PLAYFAIR	Orkney 13th c., Fife 16th c.	
PLENDERLEITH	Roxburghshire (Oxham) 13th c.	
PLUMMER, PLUMER	Kelso, to Angus 14th c.	
POLE, POLESON	Shetland 17th c.; *MACKAY*	F2
POLK, POOK	From POLLOCK	
POLLOCK, POLLOK	Renfrew and Moray 12th c., Angus 13th c.	
POLSON	Berwickshire 12th c., W. Lothian 16th c.	
POLLARD	From 'Paulson', *MACKAY*	F2
PONT	Perth 13th c., Ayr 14th c., Aberdeen 16th c.	
PONTON	Ayrshire 14th c.	
POOL, POOLE	Dundee 14th c., Dumfries etc. 17th c.	
POPE	Elgin 14th c., to Ross etc. 16th c.	
PORTEOUS	Peeblesshire 15th c.	
PORTER	Lanarkshire, Angus etc. 13th c.	
	Glenlyon; *MACNAUGHTON*	E6
POTTER	Dumbarton, Moffat 14th c. etc.	
POTTINGER	Orkney 16th c.	
POTTS, POTT	Kelso 16th c., from PHILPOT	
POW, POWE	Glasgow 16th c., Berwickshire 17th c.	
POWER	Ayrshire 16th c.	
POWRIE	Angus (Errol) 14th c.	
PRATT	Nairn etc. 13th c.; *GRANT*	H4
PRESTON	S.E. Edinburgh 13th c.	
PRETSELL, etc.	Peeblesshire (Pratshill) 16th c.	
PRIMROSE	W. Fife, to Midlothian 14th c.	
PRINGLE	Gala Water (Hoppringle) 13th c.	
PRIOR	Dundee and Perth 16th c.	
PROCTOR	Angus etc. 15th c.	
PROUDFOOT	Berwickshire 14th c., Carnwarth etc. 17th c.	
PROVAN, PROVEN	Glasgow 12th c., Strathblane 13th c.	
PRYDE	Renfrew 13th c., Fife 16th c.	
PULLAR, PULLER	Perth 14th c.	
PUNTON	Haddington 16th c., W. Lothian 17th c.	
PURCELL, PURSELL	Lanark 15th c.; *MACDONALD*	D7
PURDIE	Peeblesshire 14th c., Angus 16th c.	
PURDOM, PURDON	Liddesdale and Glasgow 15th c.	
PURVES	Berwickshire 13th c.	
PYOTT, PYE	Inverness 14th c., Fife 17th c.; *GRAHAM*	J5
QUARRIER	Dunkeld 16th c.	
QUARRY	*MACQUARRIE*	C5
QUINTON, QUENTIN	Kelso 13th c., Edinburgh etc. 17th c.	
RAE	Dumfriesshire etc. 13th c.; *MACRAE*	E4
RAEBURN	N. Ayrshire (Ryburn) 14th c.	
RAFFLES	S. Annandale (Raffles) 13th c.	

SURNAME	CLAN OR DISTRICT SOURCE	KEY TO MAP
RAINNIE, RAINY	'Ranald', W. Fife 14th c., Angus etc. 15th c., Keppoch *MACDONNELL*	F5
RAIT, RAITT	Nairn 13th c., Angus etc. 15th c.	
RAITH	Ayr (Raith) 15th c.; *MACRAE*	E4
RAMAGE	Perth 14th c., Stobo etc. 16th c.	
RAMSAY	Midlothian (Dalhousie) 12th c. (now a clan in its own right)	I7
RANDALL, RANDELL	Fife 13th c., Orkney 14th c.	
RANDOLPH	Fife, Roxburgh 13th c.; *BRUCE*	I8
RANKEILLOR	Cupar-Fife 13th c.	
RANKEN, RANKIN, RANKINE	Ayrshire 15th c.; *MACLEAN*	D6
RATTER	Caithness (Ratter), to Orkney 15th c.	
RATTRAY	Gowrie 15th c.	H6
RAY, REA	See RAE	
READ, REED	Same as REID	
READDIE, REDDIE	Angus (Reedie), to Fife 16th c.	
REAY	*MACRAE*; *MACKAY*	E4, F2
REDDEN, REDDIN	Kelso (Redden) 12th c.	
REDPATH, REIDPATH	Lauderdale (Earlston) 13th c.	
REE	From MACRIE, *MACRAE*	E4
REEKIE	Angus etc. 16th c.	
REIACH	Fife, from RIACH: *FARQUHARSON*	I5
REID, REED	Aberdeenshire, Ayrshire 14th c. Perthshire, *ROBERTSON*	H5
REIDFURD	Aberdeenshire etc. 16th c.; *INNES*	I3
REITH	From MACRAITH, *MACRAE*	E4
RENDALL, RENDLE	Same as RANDALL	
RENNIE, RENNY	From Ranald, see RAINNIE	
RENTON	Berwick (Coldingham) 13th c.	
RENWICK, RENNICK	Lanarkshire etc. 17th c.	
RETTIE	Banffshire, to Aberdeen 15th c.	
REVAN, REVANS	*MACQUEEN*	C3
REVIE	S.W. Scotland, from MACILRIACH	
RHIND, RHYND	Perthshire etc. 14th c.; *LINDSAY*	J5
RIACH, REOCH	*FARQUHARSON*; *MACDONALD*	I5, D7
RICHARDSON	Clyde 14th c.; *OGILVIE*; *BUCHANAN*	J5, F6
RIDDELL, RIDDLE	Roxburghshire, Midlothian 12th c.	
RIDLAND	Orkney (Redland), to Shetland 17th c.	
RIGG	Ayr, Dumfries etc. 16th c.	
RINTOUL	Kinross-shire, Perthshire 16th c.	
RIPLEY	Moray 13th c.; *MACINTOSH*	G4
RISK	Stirlingshire 16th c.; *BUCHANAN*	F6
RITCHIE	Border 16th c.; *MACINTOSH*	G4
ROBB	*MACFARLANE*; Appin *STEWART*	F6, E5
ROBBIE	See MACROBBIE	
ROBERTON	Lanarkshire (Roberton) 13th c.	
ROBERTS	*ROBERTSON*	G5—H5
ROBERTSON	Clan *ROBERTSON*	G5—H5
ROBISON, ROBSON	Tweed 15th c.; *GUNN*; *ROBERTSON*	H2, H5
ROBINS	*MACGREGOR*	F6
ROBINSON	Ayrshire, Glasgow 15th c.; *GUNN*	H2
ROCHE, ROCK	Edinburgh 13th c., Aberdeen 15th c.	
RODERICK	*MACDONALD*	C3, D7
RODGER, ROGER	Angus 15th c., Glasgow 16th c.	
RODGERS, RODGIE	Aberdeen 16th c., Angus etc. 17th c.	

ROGERSON, ROGERS	Aberdeen 13th c., Angus etc. 15th c.	
ROLLAND	Perthshire, Ayrshire 13th c.	
ROLLO, ROLLOCK	Perthshire 12th c. (Rollo is now a clan in its own right)	H6
ROMANES	Peeblesshire (Rommano) 13th c.	
ROME	Annandale 16th c.; *JOHNSTON*	I8
RONALD, RONALDSON	MACDONNELL of Keppoch	F5
RORIE, RORISON	*MACDONALD*; *MACLAREN*	A3−D7, G6
ROSE	Clan ROSE	H3
ROSIE, ROSEY	N.E. Caithness 17th c.	
ROSS	Clan *ROSS*; and from *ROSE*	G3, H3
ROUGH	Lanarkshire, Linlithgow 15th c.	
ROUGHHEAD	Berwickshire etc. 15th c.	
ROUSAY, ROWSAY	Orkney 17th c.	
ROWAN, ROWAND	From ROLLAND	
ROWAT, ROWATT	Glasgow 16th c.	
ROWE, ROW	Dunbartonshire (Rhu) 13th c.	
ROXBURGH	Roxburghshire etc. 12th c.	
ROY	From MACINROY; Galloway MILROY; also *MACGREGOR*	F6
RULE	Roxburghshire (Rule) 13th c.	
RUNCIMAN	Roxburghshire 15th c., Moray 16th c.	
RUSK	Strathearn, *BUCHANAN*	F6
RUSKIN	Lorne, *BUCHANAN*	F6
RUSSELL, RUSSEL	Tweedside 12th c.; *CUMMING*	G5
RUST	Aberdeenshire 16th c.	
RUTHERFORD	Roxburghshire 12th c.	J7
RUTHVEN	Angus and Perthshire 12th c.	H5
RYRIE	(MACREARIE) *MACDONALD*	D7
SADDLER, SADLER	Roxburgh 14th c., Ayr, Perth etc. 15th c.	
SALMON, SALMOND	Perthshire 15th c.	
SALTON	E. Lothian and Linlithgow 14th c.	
SAMSON, SAMPSON	Lanarkshire 16th c., Merse 17th c.	
SANDEMAN	Perthshire (Alyth) 17th c.	
SANDERS, SANDER	See SAUNDERS	
SANDERSON	*MACDONELL* of Glengarry	E4
SANDILANDS	Upper Clyde 14th c.; *DOUGLAS*	H8
SANDISON	Shetland (Sandsound) 15th c.; *GUNN*	H2
SANDS	W. Fife (Sands) 15th c.	
SANGSTER, SANG	Aberdeenshire 15th c.	
SAUNDERS	Perth 15th c. etc.; *MACDONELL* of Glengarry; *MACALISTER*	E4, D7
SAVAGE, SAVIDGE	Edinburgh, Sanquhar 17th c.	
SCALES	Dumfriesshire, Merse 17th c.	
SCARLETT	Annandale 13th c., Caithness 14th c.	
SCARTH	Orkney (Scarth) 15th c.	
SCLATER	Aberdeen 14th c., Angus etc. 15th c.	
SCOBIE, SCOBBIE	Perthshire 14th c.; *MACKAY*	F2
SCOLLAY	Orkney (Skaill) 16th c.	
SCORGIE	Aberdeenshire 17th c.	
SCOTLAND	Kinross-shire 17th c.	
SCOTT	Clan *SCOTT*	I8
SCOUGAL, SCOUGALL	E. Lothian (Scougall) 13th c.	
SCOULAR, SCOULLER	Berwickshire 16th c.	
SCRIMGEOUR	Fife and Angus 13th c. (now a clan in its own right)	

SURNAME	CLAN OR DISTRICT SOURCE	KEY TO MAP
SCROGGIE	Perthshire 15th c., Aberdeen 16th c.	
SEATH	Fife, *SHAW*	H4
SEATON	Annandale 12th c., E. Lothian 14th c.	
SEATTER, SEATER	Orkney (Setter) 16th c.	
SEGGIE	Kinross-shire (Seggie) 15th c.	
SELKIRK, SELCRAIG	Selkirk 13th c., to Edinburgh 14th c.	
SELLAR, SELLARS	Aberdeen 13th c.; from SADDLER	
SEMPLE, SEMPILL	Renfrewshire 13th c.	
SERLE	Perth 13th c.	
SERVICE	Roxburghshire, Stirling 13th c.	
SETH	Fife, *SHAW*	H4
SETON	Same as SEATON	
SHADE, SHEED	Edinburgh 16th c.	
SHAND	Aberdeenshire 16th c.	
SHANK, SHANKS	Midlothian 14th c., Lanarkshire 15th c.	
SHANNON	Galloway 14th c.; *MACDONALD*	D7
SHARP, SHARPE	Peeblesshire 14th c., Perthshire 15th c.; Bute, from MACELHERAN; *STUART*	E7
SHAW	Renfrewshire, Lanarkshire 13th c.; *SHAW*; Clan *CHATTAN*	H4
SHEACH	Moray etc.; *SHAW*	H4
SHEARER, SHERAR	Fife, Aberdeen etc. 14th c.	
SHEDDEN, SHEDDON	Renfrewshire, Ayrshire 17th c.	
SHENNAN	Same as SHANNON	
SHEPHERD	Peebles 13th c., Moray 14th c. etc.	
SHERET, SHERRATT	Dunbartonshire, Aberdeen 17th c.	
SHERIFF, SHERIFFS	Aberdeen 14th c.	
SHERRIE, SHERRY	From MACSHERRIE, *MACKINNON*	D4
SHEWAN	Aberdeen 15th c., Shetland etc. 17th c.	
SHIACH	Moray etc.; *SHAW*	H4
SHIELD, SHIELL ⎫ SHIELS, SHIELDS ⎬	Tweeddale and Midlothian 13th c., Glasgow etc. 15th c.	
SHIERLAW, SHIRLAW	Lanarkshire 15th c.	
SHILLINGLAW	Peeblesshire (Traquair) 17th c.	
SHIRRAS, SHIRREFF	See SHERIFF	
SHIVAS, SHIVES	E. Aberdeenshire (Shivas) 14th c.	
SHOOLBREAD	Fife (Auchtermuchty) 17th c.	
SHORT, SHORTT	Stirlingshire 15th c., Dumfries 17th c.	
SHORTREED	Selkirk, Kelso 17th c.	
SIBBALD	Fife etc. 13th c.	
SILVER	Angus, Mearns 15th c.	
SIM, SIME	Lanarkshire etc. 16th c.; *FRASER*	F4
SIMON, SIMONS	Perth 13th c., Aberdeen 15th c.; *FRASER*	F4, G4
SIMPSON	From SIMSON	
SIMSON, SIMS	Edinburgh etc. 15th c.; *FRASER*	F4
SINCLAIR	Clan *SINCLAIR*	I2
SINTON	E. Selkirkshire (Sinton) 13th c.	
SIVES	Haddington 17th c., from SHIVAS	
SIVEWRIGHT	Angus 16th c.; and from CRERAR	
SKAE, SKEA	Orkney (Skea) 15th c.	
SKED, SKEDD	E. Midlothian 17th c.	
SKENE, SKEEN	Clan *SKENE*	K4
SKEOCH	Glasgow etc. 16th c.	
SKIMMING	Galloway, from MACSKIMMING	
SKINNER	Aberdeen 13th c., Inverness etc. 14th c.; *MACGREGOR*	F6

SLATER, SLATTER	See SCLATER	
SLEIGH	Aberdeen 13th c.	
SLESSOR, SLESSER	Aberdeen 15th c.	
SLIMON, SLIMMAN	Perthshire 15th c., Kelso etc. 16th c.	
SLOAN, SLOANE	Midlothian, Galloway etc. 16th c.	
SLORA, SLORACH	Moray etc. 16th c.; *DAVIDSON*	G4
SMAIL, SMALE SMALL, SMEALL }	Border 14th c., Aberdeen 15th c.; *MURRAY*	H6
SMART, SMAIRT	Fife 14th c., Angus 15th c.; *MACKENZIE*	F3
SMEATON	Midlothian (Smeaton) 13th c.	
SMELLIE, SMILLIE	Lanarkshire 17th c.	
SMIBERT	Midlothian 15th c., E. Lothian 16th c.	
SMITH, SMYTHE	S.E. Scotland 13th c.; *MACPHERSON*; *MACFARLANE*	G4, F6
SNEDDON, SNEDDAN	S. Mearns (Snadoun); SNOWDEN	
SNELL	Ayrshire, Glasgow 15th c.	
SNODGRASS	Ayrshire (Irvine) 14th c.	
SNOWDEN, SNOWDON	Lauder (Snowden) etc. 17th c.	
SOMERVILLE	Lanarkshire 12th c., Roxburgh 13th c.	H7
SORBIE	Wigtownshire (Sorbie) 13th c.	
SORLEY, SORLIE	From MACSORLEY	
SOUNESS	Lauderdale and Aberdeenshire 17th c.	
SOUTAR, SOUTER	Dumfries 13th c., Perth etc. 14th c.	
SPALDING	Mearns etc. 13th c.; *MURRAY*	I5, G5
SPANKIE	Angus 15th c.	
SPARK, SPARKE	Aberdeen, Perth 15th c.	
SPEED	Angus 15th c.	
SPEEDIE, SPEEDY	Dunfermline etc. 16th c.	
SPEIRS, SPIERS	Ayrshire 15th c., Stirling 16th c.	
SPENCE, SPENS	Moray, Ayrshire etc. 13th c.; *MACDUFF*	I6
SPINK, SPINKS	Elgin 13th c., Arbroath 17th c.	
SPITTAL, SPITTEL	Dunbartonshire 14th c.; *BUCHANAN*	F6
SPORRAN	*MACDONALD*	D7
SPOTTISWOOD	Berwickshire (Gordon) 13th c.	
SPOWART	Clackmannan, Fife 17th c.	
SPROTT, SPROAT	Kirkcudbrightshire 13th c.	
SPROUL, SPREULL	Lennox 13th c.; *MACFARLANE*	F6
SPRUNT, SPROUNT	Angus 15th c.	
SQUAIR, SQUIRE	Midlothian 13th c., Fife 14th c.	
STABLES, STABLE	Angus 15th c.	
STALKER	*MACFARLANE*; *MACGREGOR*	F6
STANFORD	Glasgow 12th c., Perth 13th c.	
STANLEY	Edinburgh 15th c., Glasgow 17th c.	
STARK	Lanarkshire 16th c.; *ROBERTSON*	H5
STEEDMAN, STEDMAN	Angus, Fife etc. 16th c.	
STEEL, STEELE	Border 13th c., Edinburgh etc. 15th c.	
STEIN, STEEN	'Steven'; Ayrshire 15th c. etc.	
STENHOUSE	Falkirk 13th c., Fife 16th c.; *BRUCE*	I8
STEPHEN, STEVENS, STEPHENSON	See STEVENSON	
STEUART	*STEWART*	F7, H6
STEVENSON	Ayrshire 12th c., Moray 13th c., Angus 15th c.	
STEWART	Clan *STEWART*	F7
	STEWART of Appin	E5
	STEWART of Atholl	G5–H5
	STEWART of Galloway	H8

SURNAME	CLAN OR DISTRICT SOURCE	KEY TO MAP
STILL	Aberdeen 15th c.	
STILLIE	E. Lothian 13th c., Lanark 17th c.	
STIRLING	Stirling 12th c., Perthshire etc. 13th c.; also *MACGREGOR*	F6
STIRRAT, STIRIE	C. Ayrshire (Stair) 14th c.	
STOBIE, STOBBIE	Berwick, Perth 14th c.	
STODDART	Kirkcudbrightshire 14th c.	
STONE	Roxburghshire 13th c., Aberdeen 15th c.	
STOREY, STORRIE	Angus, Aberdeen 13th c.; *OGILVIE*	J5
STORRAR, STORER	Banffshire etc. 16th c.	
STOTT, STOUT	Aberdeen 13th c., Tweeddale 17th c.	
STOVE	Orkney (Sanday), to Shetland 17th c.	
STRACHAN	Kincardineshire (Strathachen) 11th c.	
STRANG, STRANGE	Angus 13th c., Aberdeen 14th c.	
STRATHERN	Strathearn 12th c.	H6
STRATHIE	Perthshire 13th c.	
STRATON, STRATTON	Midlothian 13th c., Aberdeen 15th c.	
STRINGER	Aberdeen 15th c.; *MACGREGOR*	F6
STRONACH	Moray etc. 15th c.	
STRUTHERS	Roxburghshire etc. 16th c.	
STUART	*STUART* of Bute; *STEWART*	E7, F7
STURROCK	Angus, Aberdeen 15th c.	
SUMMERS, SUMNER	Perth, Angus 14th c.; *LINDSAY*	J5
SUTHERLAND	Clan *SUTHERLAND*	G2
SUTTIE	E. Lothian etc. 17th c.; *GRANT*	F4
SWAN, SWANN	*MACQUEEN*; *GUNN*	C3, G2
SWANSON, SWANNEY	Caithness, Orkney, *GUNN*	G2
SWANSTON	Midlothian 13th c., Tweedside 16th c.	
SWIFT	Edinburgh 15th c.	
SWINTON	Berwickshire 11th c.	
SWORD	'Siward', S.E. Scotland 14th c.	
SYM, SYME	See SIM	
SYMINGTON	Upper Clydesdale 14th c.	
SYMON, SYMONS	See SIMON	
TAGGART	Dumfries 16th c.; *ROSS*	G3
TAINSH	*MACGREGOR*	F6
TAIT, TATE	Angus, Edinburgh 14th c., Orkney 16th c.	
TARRELL, TARRILL	Ross-shire 14th c., to *MACINTOSH*	G4
TASKER	Perthshire, Angus 17th c.	
TAWSEON, TAWSE	From MACTAVISH	
TAYLOR	Dumfries to Angus 13th c.; *CAMERON*	F5
TELFER, TELFORD	Lanarkshire etc. 14th c.	
TEMPLE	Midlothian, to E. Lothian 15th c.	
TEMPLETON	N. Ayrshire (Irvine) 13th c.	
TENNANT, TENNENT	W. Lothian 13th c., Stirling 14th c.	
TERRAS, TERRIS	Moray (Tarras) 14th c.	
TEVIOTDALE	Roxburghshire 13th c.	
THAIN, THAYNE	Banffshire 15th c., Angus 16th c.	
THALLON	S.W. Fife 16th c.	
THIN	Lauderdale etc. 16th c.	
THIRD	Aberdeen 16th c. etc.	
THOM, THOMAS	Angus etc. 15th c.; *MACTHOMAS*	I5
THOMASON	Sutherland 16th c.; *MACFARLANE*	F6
THOMPSON	From THOMSON	
THOMS	From *MACTHOMAS*; *MACINTOSH*	I5, H5

SURNAME	CLAN OR DISTRICT SOURCE	KEY TO MAP
THOMSON	Ayrshire 14th c.; *MACTHOMAS*	I5
THORBURN	Aberdeen 14th c., Tweeddale 15th c.	
THORNTON	Mearns, also Angus 13th c.	
THRIEPLAND	Peeblesshire 13th c., to Perth 17th c.	
TINDALL, TINDELL	Dumfries, Glasgow 13th c., Angus 15th c.	
TINLIN, TINLINE	Roxburghshire 17th c.	
TOD, TODD	Berwickshire 13th c.; *GORDON*	J4
TOFTS	C. Roxburghshire, (Kirkton) 13th c.	
TOLMIE	*MACLEOD* of Lewis	D4
TONNOCHY	*ROBERTSON*	G5
TOPP	Aberdeenshire 15th c.	
TORBAIN	Fife (Kirkcaldy) 16th c.	
TORRANCE	N.W. Lanarkshire (Torrance) 16th c.	
TORRIE, TORRY	Dumfriesshire 15th c.; *CAMPBELL*	H4, E6
TOSH, TOSHACH	*MACINTOSH* of Glentilt	H5
TOSSACK	*MACGREGOR*	F6
TOUCHE, TOUGH	Aberdeenshire 14th c., Fife 16th c.	
TOWARD, TOWART	*LAMONT*	E7
TOWERS	Edinburgh 14th c.	
TOWNS	Edinburgh 15th c., Linlithgow 16th c.	
TRAIL, TRAILL	Fife, Aberdeen 14th c., Orkney 16th c.	
TRAIN	Ayrshire 15th c.; *MACDONALD*	D7
TRAQUAIR	Peeblesshire 13th c.	
TRENCH	Berwickshire 16th c.	
TROTTER	Berwickshire and Edinburgh 14th c.	
TROUP	Ayrshire 13th c., Banff 14th c.; *GORDON*	J4
TUDHOPE	Jedburgh, to Lanark etc. 17th c.	
TULLIS	Fife 16th c.	
TULLOCH, TULLO	Angus etc. 14th c.; *ROSS*	G3
TULLY, TULLIE	Aberdeenshire 16th c. etc.	
TURCAN	W. Fife 17th c.	
TURNBULL	Teviotdale etc. 14th c.	J8
TURNER	Aberdeen 14th c., Ayrshire 15th c.; *LAMONT*	E7
TURPIE, TURPIN	'Thorfinn', Angus 13th c., Fife 17th c.	
TWADDLE	From TWEEDDALE	
TWATT	Orkney 16th c., also Shetland 17th c.	
TWEEDDALE	Tweed 14th c.; *FRASER*; *HAY*	F4, I6
TWEEDIE, TWEEDY	Lanarkshire 13th c., Tweed 14th c.; *FRASER*	F4
TYRE	From *MACINTYRE*, also MACTIRE	
TYRIE	Perthshire 13th c., to Angus etc. 15th c.	
UNDERWOOD	Ayrshire (Symington) 15th c.	
URE	Midlothian 13th c.; also MACIVER	
URIE, URRY	Clan *URQUHART*	G3
URQUHART	Ayrshire, also Mearns 13th c.; *KEITH*	J5
USHER	Angus 15th c., Peeblesshire 15th c.	
VALENTINE	Kincardineshire 14th c.	
VALLANCE	Angus 12th c., Fife 13th c.	
VASS	E. Lothian 12th c.; *MUNRO*; *ROSS*	G3
VEITCH, VETCH	Peeblesshire 13th c.	
VERT, VERTH	Edinburgh 17th c.	
VICKERS, VICARS	Roxburghshire 13th c.	
WADDELL, WADDEL	Wedale (Stow) etc. 13th c.	
WAITT, WAITE	Angus 14th c., Tweedside 16th c.	

SURNAME	CLAN OR DISTRICT SOURCE	KEY TO MAP
WAKE	Dumfriesshire 14th c., Edinburgh 15th c.	
WALDIE, WADDIE	Kelso 12th c., Aberdeen 14th c.	
WALKER	Galloway, Inverness etc. 14th c.	
	Same as MACNUCATOR	
WALKINGSHAW	Renfrewshire 13th c.	
WALLACE, WALLIS	Ayrshire, Renfrewshire 12th c.	F7
WALLS	Orkney 15th c.; also from WALLACE	F7
WALSH	Same as WELSH	
WALTER, WALTERS	Galloway, Fife, Aberdeen 14th c.;	F6, J4
	BUCHANAN; *FORBES*	
WANLESS, WANLISS	W. Lothian 16th c., Angus 17th c.	
WANN	Edinburgh, Glasgow etc. 15th c.	
WARD	Peeblesshire 14th c., Stirling 17th c.	
WARDEN	Angus, Fife etc. 17th c.	
WARDLAW	Fife 11th c., Roxburghshire 14th c.	
WARDROP	Fife and Midlothian 13th c.	
WARE	Same as WEIR	
WARES	N.E. Caithness; *SINCLAIR*	I2
WARNOCK	'Macilvernock', Galloway 12th c.	
WARRACK	Aberdeenshire 15th c., Edinburgh 16th c.	
WARREN	W. Fife 13th c.	
WARWICK	Ayrshire etc. 13th c.	
WASS	Same as VASS	
WATERS	From WALTERS	
WATERSTON	Angus, Midlothian etc. 14th c.	
WATSON, WASON	*BUCHANAN*; *FORBES*	F6, J4
WATT, WATTERS	'Walter': *FORBES*; *BUCHANAN*	J4, F6
WATTIE, WATTS	Aberdeenshire, *FORBES*	J4
WAUCHOPE	Dumfriesshire, Midlothian 11th c.	
WAUGH	From WAUCHOPE, Roxburghshire 13th c.	
WEATHERHEAD	Lauderdale 15th c.	
WEATHERSTONE	Lauderdale 17th c., from WATERSTON	
WEBSTER, WEAVER	Stirling etc. 15th c.; *MACFARLANE*	F6
WEDDELL, WEDDLE	Same as WADDELL	
WEDDERBURN	Berwickshire 13th c., Dundee 15th c.; HOME;	J7
	SCRIMGEOUR	
WEIR	Lanarkshire 12th c.; and from MACNUIR	
WELIVER	*MACGREGOR*	F6
WELLS	Fife and Aberdeenshire 13th c.	
WELSH, WELCH	Tweedside 14th c.	
WEMYSS, WEEMS	Fife 12th c.; *MACDUFF* (Wemyss is now a clan	I6
	in its own right)	
WEST	Perthshire, Buchan etc. 17th c.	
WESTON	Lanarkshire, Wigtown etc. 13th c.	
WESTWATER	W. Fife 16th c.	
WESTWOOD	Fife 15th c.	
WHAMOND	'Quhoman', Banff 15th c.	
WHANNEL	Galloway, see MACWHANNELL	
WHARRIE	Lanarkshire, from *MACQUARRIE*	C5
WHEELAN, WHELLAN	Argyll 16th c.; *MACDONALD*	D7
WHIGHAM	Peebles 15th c., Lothians 16th c.	
WHITE, WHYTE	Angus 13th c., Ayrshire etc. 14th c.;	E7, F6
	LAMONT; *MACGREGOR*	
WHITECROSS	Aberdeenshire 16th c.	
WHITEFORD	Renfrewshire 13th c.	
WHITEHEAD	Berwick 13th c., W. Lothian 16th c.	

WHITELAW	Roxburghshire, Midlothian 13th c.	
WHITSON	Perthshire 14th c., Angus 15th c.	
WHITTEN, WHITTON	Roxburghshire 12th c.	
WHYMAN	Peebles 14th c., and as WHAMOND	
WHYTOCK	Edinburgh 16th c.	
WIGHT	Perth 13th c., E. Lothian 16th c.	
WIGHTMAN	Peeblesshire etc. 16th c.	
WIGHTON	Angus 15th c.	
WILCOX	*MACGREGOR*	F6
WILKIE	Midlothian 14th c., also from MACQUILKAN	
WILKINSON	Lanarkshire 15th c., also from MACQUILKAN	
WILL, WILLS	Aberdeen 15th c.; *GUNN*	H2
WILLIS, WILLISON	Dumfries 13th c., Lanarkshire 17th c.	
WILLIAMSON	Fife 12th c., Peebles 14th c.; *MACKAY,*	F2
	also from MACWILLIAM	
WILLOCKS, WILLOX	Aberdeen 16th c.; also *MACGREGOR*	F6
WILSON	Ayrshire etc. 15th c.; *GUNN*	H2
WINDRAM, WINRAM	Lanarkshire 15th c., Fife etc. 16th c.	
WINCHESTER	Ayrshire, Lanarkshire 13th c.	
WINGATE, WINZET	Glasgow 16th c.	
WINNING	Ayrshire etc. 13th c.	
WINTON, WINTOUN	E. Lothian 12th c., Aberdeen etc. 14th c.	
WINTOUR, WINTERS	Selkirkshire 12th c., Glasgow etc. 15th c.	
WISEMAN	Moray 13th c., Aberdeenshire 14th c.	
WISHART	Kincardineshire etc. 13th c.	
WOOD	Nairnshire 13th c., Dumfriesshire 14th c.	
WOODBURN	Ayrshire 16th c.	
WORKMAN	Dunfermline 16th c. etc.	
WOTHERSPOON	Renfrew 13th c., Fife etc. 16th c.	
WRIGHT	Stirlingshire etc. 13th c.; *MACINTYRE*	E6
WYATT	Angus 13th c.	
WYLIE, WYLLIE	Dumfriesshire 14th c.; *GUNN*;	H2
	MACFARLANE	F6
WYSE	Moray etc. 14th c., Stirling 15th c.	
YATES, YEATS	Dumfriesshire 14th c., Angus 15th c.	
YEAMAN, YEOMAN	Moray, Dundee 16th c.	
YELLOWLEES	Fife 15th c., Berwickshire 16th c.	
YORKSTON, YORSTON	Edinburgh and Orkney 15th c.	
YOUNG	Moray, Angus etc. 14th c.	
YOUNGER	Fife etc. 14th c.	
YOUNGSON	Aberdeenshire 16th c.	
YOUNNIE, YUNNIE	Moray 17th c.	
YOURSTON	From YORKSTON	
YUILL, YULE, YOOL	Aberdeen etc. 14th c.; *BUCHANAN*	F6
ZUILL	See YUILL, *BUCHANAN*	F6

CLANS OF SCOTLAND

Alphabetically arranged, with lists of traditional septs and including the more common name variations and the names of dependent or associated families.

Definition of the word 'Clan'

The Gaelic word for 'children' is more accurately translated as 'family' in the sense in which the word *clan* became accepted in the Scottish Highlands during the 13th century. A clan is a social group whose core comprises a number of families derived from, or accepted as being derived from, a common ancestor. Almost without exception, that core is accompanied by a further number of dependent and associated families who have either sought the protection of the clan at some point in history or have been tenants or vassals of its chief. That chief is owed allegiance by all members of the clan, but ancient tradition nevertheless states that 'the Clan is above the Chief'. Although Gaelic has been supplanted by English in the Lowlands of Scotland for nearly a thousand years, it is an acceptable convention to refer to the great Lowland families, like the Douglases, as clans, although the heads of certain families, such as Bruce, prefer not to use the term.

Allegiance was generally given to a father's clan, but Celtic tradition includes a strong element of descent through, and loyalty to, a mother's line. In reality, the chief of a clan would 'ingather' any stranger — of whatever family — who possessed suitable skills, maintained his allegiance and, if required, adopted the clan surname.

CLAN ALPIN   Tradition claims MacAlpin or MacAlpine as the oldest and most purely Celtic of the Highland clans, of royal descent from the dynasty of Kenneth MacAlpin who united Picts and Scots into one kingdom from the year 850 and transferred his capital to Perthshire from Dun Add in Dalriada (beside Loch Crinan). However, no clan of the name survived into the heyday of the clan system, though individual MacAlpins are recorded from the 13th century, mostly then in Perthshire. Clan MacGregor claims origin from that royal MacAlpin stock: as also do MacAulay, MacDuff, MacFie, MacKinnon, MacNab and MacQuarrie.

ARMSTRONG (Map J8)   This variation of the Norman name Fortinbras has been known in the West Marches since the 13th century. Before the Union of the Crowns in 1603, this small border clan found themselves in an area of sharp contention, and the Armstrong chiefs adopted a traditional right of wide foray and tribute-levying into the 'Auld Enemy's' territory. At length, such diplomatic embarrassments from his over-active subjects moved James V to suppress them in 1529 by an expedition disguised as a great hunting tour. Several border ballads recount the aggrieved shock of 'Johnnie Armstrong of Gilknockie' and other leaders preparing to welcome their sovereign and finding themselves facing the hangman instead. That not all the clan were alike is obvious from the Gilbert Armstrong who was High Steward to King David II and his ambassador to England.

Septs:

CROSIER	FAIRBAIRN	NIXON
CROZER	GROZIER	

BRODIE (Map H3)   Early records were destroyed by Lord Gordon, when he burned Brodie Castle, Nairnshire, in 1645; but the de Brothies or Brodies are elsewhere mentioned in influential positions from at least the 14th century. Whether an ancient tribe secured in loyal possession or related to the incoming Murrays, the Brodie name and lands became established when Malcolm IV transplanted other rebelling Moray tribes to different districts, about 1165.

Septs:

BRODY	BRYDE	BRYDIE

BRUCE (Map I8, F8)   With the representatives of Norman families who accompanied William the Conqueror, those of de Brus, Robert and his two sons, were not far behind. In the name of Brusi, another branch directly Norse had already acquired a share of the Orkney earldom.

Robert's second son, Adam, acquired large territories in Yorkshire, and Adam's son Robert was one of the friends of the Scottish King David I who accompanied him at his accession in 1124, when returning from his sojourn in England. This Robert de Brus was granted the lordship of Annandale with the hand of that district's native heiress. The seventh of the Brus lords of Annandale, Robert de Brus (1274-1329, and later often called 'The Bruce'), was to become King Robert I, the victor of Bannockburn and liberator of Scotland.

From his mother, the heiress of Carrick, Turnberry Castle became a new nucleus of the Bruces; then from 1359 another branch spread still more extensively from Clackmannan into Fife and elsewhere. From Kinnaird, on the Forth shore opposite, came James Bruce (1730-94), who displayed gifts more versatile and diplomatic than are suggested by a bare reminder of his Abyssinian adventures and first exploration of the Nile sources.

Septs:

CARLYLE	CROSBIE	STENHOUSE
CARRUTHERS	RANDOLPH	

BUCHANAN (Map F6)   Legend derives the clan's original name MacAuslan from Irish prince Anselan O Kyan, granted a settlement in Lennox by Malcolm II. The Auselan first actually recorded was steward to a 13th-century Earl of Lennox, from whom he obtained the Loch-Lomondside district of Buchanan, which includes Ben Lomond. His son Gilbert was the first user of the Buchanan surname, as well as founder of the branches that took his name. From Gilbert's brothers Colman and Methlan, grandson Maurice and great-grandson Walter, there derived other sept names and the separated clan MacMillan.

George Buchanan, a forerunner (though in Latin) of Burns and Byron, the tutor of Montaigne, Mary Queen of Scots and James VI, historian and Reformationist, ranks as the clan's chief personality, though a U.S. President could be among others cited.

Septs:

COLMAN	LENNIE	MACCHRUITER	MACKINLEY
CORMACK	LENNY	MACCOLMAN	MACMASTER
COUSLAND	MACALDONICH	MACCORMACK	MACMAURICE
DEWAR	MACALMAN	MACCUBBIN	MACMURCHIE
DOVE	MACASLAN	MACCUBING	MACMURCHY
DOW	MACASLIN	MACCUBIN	MACNEUR
GIBB	MACAUSELAN	MACGEORGE	MACNUIR
GIBBON	MACAUSLAN	MACGIBBON	MACNUYER
GIBSON	MACAUSLAND	MACGREUSICH	MACQUATTIE
GILBERT	MACAUSLANE	MACGUBBIN	MACWATTIE
GILBERTSON	MACCALMAN	MACINALLY	MACWHIRTER
HARPER	MACCALMONT	MACINDEOR	MASTERS
HARPERSON	MACCAMMOND	MACINDOE	MASTERSON
LEAVY	MACCASLAND	MACKINLAY	MORRICE

MORRIS	RUSK	WASON	YUILL
MORRISON	RUSKIN	WATERS	YOOL
MURCHIE	SPITTAL	WATSON	YULE
MURCHISON	SPITTEL	WATT	ZUILL
RICHARDSON	WALTER	WATTERS	
RISK	WALTERS	WEIR	

CAMERON (Map F5) The clan, settled in Lochaber since at least Bruce's time, later became an important branch of the Clan Chattan confederacy, and their name, taken as *Cam-shorn*('s' silent), 'hook-nose', is reported to have fitted many Highland Camerons. But Camerons also, from the Norman name Cambron, had for a century before Bruce been spreading widely from their Fife headquarters of the same name. If the name in common is more coincidence, it is not the only one.

Among several branches of the Highland clan, that of the Chief acquired their Lochiel property by marriage and made that name, with their motto 'For King and Country', resound in the Stewart causes. Then in 1793 under Cameron of Erracht they founded the 79th or Cameron Highlanders to serve with no less distinction.

The southern Camerons of the 17th century directed their zeal rather differently. The scholarly John Cameron founded a protestant group in France called Cameronites; Richard Cameron, killed at Airdsmoss, 1680, a militant Covenanter, gave his name to the Cameronian sect and a later Lowland regiment.

Septs:

CHALMERS	KENNEDY	MACILDOWIE	MACSORLEY
CHAMBERS	LEARY	MACKAIL	MACULRIG
CLARK	LONIE	MACKELL	MACVAIL
CLARKE	MACALDOWIE	MACLEAR	MACWALRICK
CLARKSON	MACALONIE	MACCLEARY	MARTIN
CLEARY	MACCHLERY	MACLERIE	PAUL
CLERK	MACCLAIR	MACMARTIN	SORLEY
DOWIE	MACLEARY	MACONIE	SORLIE
GIBBON	MACGILLERY	MACOSTRICH	TAYLOR
GILBERTSON	MACGILLONIE	MACPHAIL	

CAMPBELL (Map F6, G6, G7) Like their name itself, frequently interpreted as *Cambeul*, 'wry-mouth', this forthrightly ambitious clan claims origins both Celtic and Norman, though the accounts vary. One relates how Malcolm of the clan, anciently named O'Duibhne or MacDiarmid, went as a widower to Norman France where he married an heiress of the Beauchamp family and adopted that name. A son, Archibald, accompanied the Conqueror in 1066 and became founder to several English lines, these ringing changes on the name, as Beauchamp to Beecham, Campobello to Kemble. Hugo de Morville, David I's High Constable and assistant feudaliser, married Beatrix de Campobello and introuced Campbells as vassals on his Ayrshire lands.

Of their main stem, rising to its dukedom of Argyll, we hear of them in possession at Lochow (Loch Awe) after Alexander II's conquest of Argyll. This need not contradict the other tradition of Lochow as O'Duibhne territory from long earlier. It would clinch with the Campbell aptitude for backing the winning authority, and with their later royal commission of 1614-17 to suppress the refractory MacDonalds and oust them from Kintyre. The troublesome MacGregors of Perthshire had just previously been treated to a similar policing. And Highland memories run deep. Among many Campbell branches, that of Breadalbane illustrates their other aptitude for successful marriage, being begun by a 14th-century match with the Glenorchy heiress. For other septs, see Campbell of Cawdor, also MacArthur.

Thomas Campbell (1777-1844) was author of many rousing ballads, including 'Lochiel's Warning', 'Lord Ullin's Daughter', and 'Battle of the Baltic'.

Septs:

BALLANTYNE	KISSOCK	MACGLASRICH	MACORAN
BANNATYNE	LORNE	MACGUBBIN	MACPHEDRAN
BURNES	LOUDEN	MACISAAC	MACQUAKER
BURNESS	LOWDON	MACIVER	MACTAUSE
BURNS	LOWDEN	MACIVOR	MACTAVISH
CONNOCHIE	LOUDON	MACKELLAR	MACTHOMAS
CONOCHIE	MACCOLM	MACKELVIE	MACURE
DENOON	MACCOMBE	MACKERLICH	MACVICAR
DENUNE	MACCONACHIE	MACKERLIE	OCHILTREE
DONACHIE	MACCONCHIE	MACKESSACK	ORR
DONAGHY	MACCONNECHY	MACKESSOCK	PATERSON
FISHER	MACCURE	MACKISSOCK	PINKERTON
HAWES	MACDERMID	MACKIVER	TAWESON
HAWS	MACDERMONT	MACLAWS	TAWSE
HAWSON	MACDIARMID	MACLEHOSE	THOMAS
ISAAC	MACDONACHIE	MACLIVER	THOMPSON
ISAACS	MACELLAR	MACNICHOL	THOMSON
IVERSON	MACELVIE	MACNICOL	URE
KELLAR	MACEUR	MACNIVEN	
KELLER	MACEVER	MACNOCAIRD	
KISSACK	MACGIBBON	MACONACHIE	

CAMPBELL of Cawdor (Map G4) The Calder or Cawdor family and name derive from Hugh de Cadella and his heirs, who gave valuable service to King Malcolm Canmore and his successors and were awarded the Nairnshire thaneship which is notably mentioned in Shakespeare's *Macbeth*. In 1493 this fell to an infant heiress, Muriel, and James IV appointed as wards her uncle, a Rose of Kilravock, and the Earl of Argyll. The latter sent an expedition which contrived to abduct Muriel as a young child to Inveraray, where in 1510 she married the Earl's third son, Sir John Campbell, and thus gave that clan a northern foothold.

Septs:

	CADDELL	CALDER	TORRIE
	CADELL	CATTELL	TORRY

CLAN CHATTAN This long-powerful group of clans comprised two main divisions, respectively under Macintosh and MacPherson leadership, with some subsidiary septs and family groups joining for protection under a geneal banner. Dissension arose among the sections from various causes, not least from their encroaching neighbours, the Gordons, enticing them into opposing camps, as at Harlaw in 1411.

Accounts of the Clan Chattan's origin vary. The Macintoshes, holding to their own Macduff origin, regard it as a confederacy, with the MacPhersons just a branch from Macintosh stock. MacPhersons, putting reliance on a written genealogy of 1450, favour the Chattan sections as having branched from an ancestor, Gillechattan Mor, a Moray chief of the early 11th century, his elder son Nechtan founding the MacPhersons and the younger, Neil, the Macintoshes, which surname only appears two centuries later. Either way of it, the Clunie MacPhersons retained the old Chattan chiefship, although in 1291 the Macintoshes, through marriage of their chief Angus to Eva, the MacPherson heiress, achieved the greater share of land and followers and also their chief's right to be styled 'Captain of the Clan Chattan', leaving their claim to full chiefship a good-going dispute scarcely yet settled.

Septs:

MacPherson Group	Macintosh Group	
MACPHERSON	MACINTOSH	MACHARDIE
DAVIDSON	FARQUHARSON	MACQUEEN
GILLESPIE	MACBEAN	NOBLE
KEITH	MACGILLIVRAY	MACTAVISH
SMITH	MACGLASHAN	SHAW

Also: CAMERON, CATTANACH, CLARK, MACPHAIL

CHISHOLM (Map F4)   Originally Normans, the Chisholm or Chisholme family took name from the lands of Cheseholm that they occupied in Roxburghshire from the 13th century or earlier. It was through marriages with northern heiresses that they established themselves a Highland clan, and Sir Robert de Cheseholme became in 1359 Constable of the royal castle of Urquhart. Erchless Castle, Strathglass, remains the ancestral seat of their chief.

COLQUHOUN (Map F6)   The lands of Colquhoun (pronounced 'Cohoon') by Loch Lomond, were granted by a 13th-century Earl of Lennox to Humphrey de Kilpatrick or Kirkpatrick, from whom the clan take descent. In the following century the neighbouring lands of Luss were included through Sir Robert Colquhoun's marrying their heiress. The last inter-clan battle, in Glenfruin nearby, in 1603, was the culmination of the long feud between the Colquhouns and MacGregors and led to the outlawry of the latter by royal command.

Septs:

COWAN	KIRKPATRICK	MACCOWAN	MACMANUS
COWEN	LAING	MACLINDEN	MACOWAN
INGRAM	MACACHOUNICH	MACLINTOCK	
KILPATRICK	MACCLINTOCK	MACMAINS	

CUMMING (Map G5)   The Cummings or Cumyns trace Norman descent from Charlemagne through Robert de Comyn, appointed governor of Northumberland in 1068 by his kinsman, William the Conqueror. Under David I, William de Comyn became Chancellor of Scotland in 1133. Settled first in Roxburghshire, the family later gained through marriages the earldoms of Buchan and Badenoch, and Altyre in Moray has long been the seat of their chief. From 1309 the Comyns' power was broken through their having contested Bruce's succession to the throne. Sir John ('the Red') Comyn's mother was the sister of ex-king John Baliol. He was slain by Bruce's party at Dumfries (Map I8), and the Buchan Comyns were defeated in battle at Inverurie, 1308.

Septs:

BUCHAN	COMMON	CUMMINGS	MACNIVEN
CHEYNE	COMMONS	CUMYN	NIVEN
CHIENE	CUMMIN	FARQUHARSON	RUSSELL

DAVIDSON (Map G4)   The clan MacDhai or Davidson, earliest settled at Invernahaven in Strathspey, are believed to take name from an ancestor, David Dhu, fourth son of Murriach, the 12th-century founder of the MacPhersons. Members of the Clan Chattan, they were deeply involved in the quarrels of precedency that beset that confederacy. These were publicly culminated in 1396 in the famous thirty-a-side combat MacPherson v. Davidson, before King Robert III and his court on the North Inch of Perth. Whether because 29 leading MacDhais were killed, or because one escaped alive, the clan thereafter fell from prominence. They are now chiefly represented by the Davidsons of Tulloch in Cromarty. A small border clan Davidson arose in Roxburghshire around the 16th century, perhaps of quite independent origin, like the Davie name in Orkney, and others. The Inverness-shire MacKays are really MacDhais.

Septs:

DAVEY	DEA	DOW	MACDADE
DAVIE	DEAN	DYE	MACDAID
DAVIS	DEANE	KAY	MACDAVID
DAVISON	DEAS	KEAY	MACKAY
DAWSON	DEASON	KEY	SLORA
DAY	DEY	KEYS	SLORACH

DOUGLAS (Map H8, J5)   An adequate history of the Douglases would be largely one of Scotland itself, where they long rivalled the royal power and eleven times married into it. Perhaps originally kinsmen of Freskin, the Clan Murray founder, it is in the south that they first come to note. Here in the 12th century they originated the 'Black Douglases' — of Douglasdale (Lanarkshire), Dumfriesshire, and Galloway. The next century saw the 'Red Douglases' established at Dalkeith (whence sprang the Earls of Morton), and then in Angus. The term 'Black Douglas' was first applied by the English to the Sir James who was Bruce's doughty lieutenant, to fall at last in Spain when on his final service of conveying the royal heart to the Holy Land.

Septs:

CAVERS	FORREST	LOCKERBY	SANDILANDS
DOUGLASS	GLENDINNING	MACGUFFIE	
DRYSDALE	INGLIS	MACGUFFOCK	
FOREST	KIRKPATRICK	MORTON	

DRUMMOND (Map H6)   The name is from the clan's earliest land at Drymen, near Loch Lomond, conferred, a tradition says, upon their ancestor Maurice who married Queen Margaret's maid-of-honour; adding that either he or his father was the Hungarian prince who piloted the refugee vessel of 1066 that brought Malcolm Canmore's bride-to-be. The earliest chief now documented was Malcolm Beg, or 'the little', a 13th-century Steward to the Earl of Lennox.

The Drummond arms display a motto, 'Gang warily', and the caltrops, those four-spiked cavalry snags that a later Sir Malcolm contributed to the victory of Bannockburn. For his services, Bruce awarded the lands in Perthshire where chiefly the clan was to flourish. Annabella Drummond became Queen to Robert II, the first Stewart king; and from then on to the last Stewart, no clan remained more faithfully adherent than the Drummonds.

Septs:

BEGG	GREWAR	MACGROUTHER	MACROBIE
BREWER	GRUAR	MACGRUDER	MUSHET
CARGILL	GRUER	MACGRUER	ROBBIE
DOCK	MACCROUTHER	MACGRUTHER	
DOIG	MACGREWAR	MACROBBIE	

ELLIOT (Map J8)   The surname appears in the 13th century, both in England (from the Old English forename Elwald) and in Scotland at Arbirlot (Aber-Eliot). Induced by the Douglases about 1395 to remove from their Angus riverside and strengthen the Border in Liddesdale, the Elliots became from there a wide-spreading clan. The names varied with different branches, as the Elliots of Minto and Eliotts of Stobs. Gilbert Elliot (1751-1814), first Earl Minto, was among the greatest of India's governors-general. His Jacobite aunt Jane Elliot penned the Flodden lament 'The Flowers o' the Forest'.

FARQUHARSON (Map I5) A branch of Clan Chattan, the Aberdeenshire Farquharsons or MacEarachers descend from Farquhar, son of the Shaw Macintosh of Rothiemurchus, Strathspey, who was awarded lands in Braemar by Bruce for assistance against the northern Comyns. No such motive could be ascribed the clan for their devotion to the Stewart causes in after centuries. From Farquhar's grandson Finlay comes MacKinlay and some other sept names. The clan extended well into Perthshire, but MacEarachers etc. of around Argyll are of Lamont or other origin.

Septs:

BARRIE	FINDLAY	KERRACHER	MACHARDIE
BOWMAN	FINDLAYSON	LYON	MACHARDY
CHRISTIE	FINLAISON	MACARTNEY	MACKERCHAR
CHRISTISON	FINLAY	MACCAIG	MACKERRACHER
CHRISTY	FINLAYSON	MACCARDNEY	MACKINDLAY
COATES	GRACIE	MACCARTNEY	MACKINLAY
COATS	GRASSICK	MACCUAIG	MACKINLEY
COUTTS	GREUSACH	MACEARACHER	PATERSON
CROMAR	HARDIE	MACERCHAR	REIACH
FARQUHAR	HARDY	MACERRACHER	REOCH
FERRIES	KELLAS	MACFARQUHAR	RIACH

FERGUSON (Map I5) Fergus was the favourite name in Gaelic-speaking Scotland, after the founder of Dalriada (now roughly Argyll).

MacFerguses, Fergus-sons, or Fergusons thus arose in areas widely dispersed. The Ayrshire Fergussons probably take name, and perhaps descent, from Fergus, the wellnigh independent 12th-century lord of Galloway; they were certainly established in the southwest before their charter from Bruce. Annie Laurie of the song became the wife of a Dumfriesshire Fergusson. Robert Fergusson (1750-74), a forerunner and inspirer of Burns, came of the Aberdeenshire clan, known there since the 14th century; and his contemporary, Adam Ferguson, the social historian, was of the Atholl branch.

Septs:

FERGIE	FERRIES	KIDDIE	MACKEDDIE
FERGUS	FORGIE	MACADIE	MACKERRAS
FERGUSSON	KEDDIE	MACFERGUS	MACKERSEY

FORBES (Map J4, K3) In its Aberdeenshire home the name is still pronounced with two syllables and is from the lands of Forbois or Forbes, granted by Alexander III to one Duncan. His son Alexander de Forbes was slain in 1304 after a long defence of Urquhart Castle (Moray) against Edward I; and his son, also Alexander, in 1332 at Dupplin Moor. Duncan Forbes (1685-1747), Lord President of the Court of Session and skilful opponent to both Jacobite rebellions from a patriotism no less sincere, matched cool wisdom against impulsive ardour and tempered justice with all the mercy he could wring from a prejudiced government.

Septs:

BANNERMAN	LUMSDEN	MEKIE	WATERS
BERRIE	MACOUAT	MELDRUM	WATSON
BERRY	MACOWAT	MICHIE	WATT
BOYCE	MACQUATTIE	MIDDLETON	WATTERS
BOYES	MACWATT	WALTER	WATTIE
FORDYCE	MECHIE	WALTERS	WATTS

FRASER (Map G4, F4, K3, K4)   At first de Friselle or Fresel, then 'Fraisier' from the *fraises*, or strawberry flowers, in their armorial bearings, this Norman family first settled in Tweeddale under Malcolm Canmore to become the chief power in Peeblesshire throughout the 12th and 13th centuries, owning Oliver, Neidpath and other castles, also estates in East Lothian. The chief male line there dying out, it devolved upon the Lovat branch which had firmly established itself in the north in Bruce's time. A further branch of Philorth founded Fraserburgh in the 16th century.

The Fraser clan have played a full part in history, not only in Scotland. For his Jacobite activities, Simon Fraser (Lord Lovat) was beheaded after Culloden at the age of eighty; and a later namesake explored the Fraser river of Canada. Sir James Frazer, author of *The Golden Bough*, made folklore a study of the modern scientist.

Septs:

ABERNETHY	GILRUTH	MACKIMMIE	SIMS
BISSET	GREWAR	MACSIMON	SIMSON
BISSETT	GRUAR	MACSYMON	SYM
BREWSTER	GRUER	MACTAVISH	SYME
COWIE	MACGREWAR	OLIVER	SYMON
FRAZER	MACGRUER	SIM	SYMONS
FRESER	MACILLRICK	SIME	TWADDLE
FREZEL	MACILRIACH	SIMON	TWEEDDALE
FRISELL	MACIMMEY	SIMONS	TWEEDIE
FRIZELLE	MACKIM	SIMPSON	

GAYRE of Gayre and Nigg arose in Cornwall in the 12th century. One branch settled in Yorkshire in the 15th century and crossed into Scotland in the 16th century and held lands in Nigg in Ross-shire. They rapidly multiplied and became landowners throughout Easter Ross. A small clan, it was recognised by Lord Lyon earlier this century.

Septs:

GAIR	GAYRE	MCGAIR	GARSON
GAIRE	GAIRN	MCGEIR	KERRISON
GEAR	GEIR	GARRISON	MCGIRR

GORDON (Map I4, J4, K4)   The 'Gay Gordons', also the name Huntly, had their Scottish origin in the Berwickshire lands of Gordon. Here, as a Norman family, they became settled under David I and retained estates for three centuries. Sir Adam de Gordon was one of the ambassadors who conveyed to the Pope the 1320 Declaration of National Independence, the first of its kind. For this and other services, Bruce granted him land of the forfeited Cummings at Strathbogie in Aberdeenshire. From that centre the Gordons came to exert great power (their chief was often called 'The Cock of the North') and were much in feud with neighbouring clans, quite often on the side of governmental stability. They founded in 1777 and 1794 the regiments that became the Gordon Highlanders.

Individuals have achieved mark in many ways, as 'Chinese Gordon', slain at Khartoum in 1885, and Lord Byron, the poet of freedom and love, a Gordon on his mother's side. Three Gordons have separately compiled works treasured for depicting Old Scotland, such as her first great Atlas of 1654.

Septs:

ADAM	ADIE	ATKINS	CROMB
ADAMS	AITCHISON	ATKINSON	CROMBIE
ADAMSON	AIKEN	BARRIE	CULLEN
ADDIE	AITKEN	CONNON	DARG
ADDISON	ATKIN	CRAIG	DARGE

DORWARD	GARRICK	LAWRIE	MOIR
DUFF	GARRIOCK	LENG	MORE
DURWARD	GEDDES	MARR	MORRICE
EADIE	GERRIE	MAVER	MORRIS
EDDIE	HUNTLY	MAVOR	MUIR
EDIE	JESSIMAN	MELDRUM	MYLNE
EDISON	JOPP	MILL	TOD
ESSLEMONT	JUPP	MILLS	TODD
GARDINER	LAING	MILN	TROUP
GARDNER	LANG	MILNE	
GARIOCH	LAURIE	MILNES	

GRAHAM (Map I7, J5, G6)   William de Graham, perhaps a native Scot, was granted by David I the Lothian lands of Abercorn and Dalkeith. His great-grandson Henry, marrying the Eskdale heiress of Avenel, established a contingent on the west Border, though the direct line died out there. The Montrose branch sprang from a different grandson of William, Sir David de Graham, who settled in Angus under William the Lion. His eldest son acquired by marriage the Strathearn district that gave name to the Menteith branch. This is unconnected with Wallace's supposed betrayer, who at least did sign the 1320 Declaration of Independence, besides three Grahams.

The 'Gallant Grahams' often enter Scottish history, most notably in the 17th century when 'the Great Marquis' (Montrose) and 'Bonnie Dundee', forty years apart, each led valorously, and met death in, the royalist cause.

Graham of Montrose Septs:

BONAR	BONNAR	GRAHAME

Graham of Menteith Septs:

AIRTH	BUNTAIN	MACGIBBON	MONTEITH
ALLARDYCE	BUNTING	MACGILVERNOCK	PYE
BLAIR	GRAHAME	MACGRIME	PYOTT
BONTEIN	HADDEN	MENTEITH	
BONTINE	HALDANE	MONTEATH	

GRANT (Map H4, F4)   Despite Gaelic interpretations, the name is simply from the French *Grand*, either 'Big' or 'Eminent', and the family was known in their original Normandy with the motto 'Stand fast!' Introduced to Scotland by marriage with the Inverness-shire Bissets, Gregory le Grant was Sheriff of that territory before 1250 and laird in Stratherrick, northeast of Loch Ness, whilst his son Lawrence, by marrying a Comyn heiress, acquired Strathspey lands that thereafter became their home country. The Glenmoriston branch was a 16th-century offshoot; and they, as indeed most of the clan, Norman in name only, adhered loyally to the Stewarts, though the Grant chiefs always favoured the ruling government.

Of General Ulysses Grant, U.S. President 1868-76, it was wagered his 'poker face' could not be tricked into emotion. But when a clansman called the old slogan 'Stand fast, Craigellachie!' (a Speyside crag), the forfeit had to be surrendered, with smiles all round.

Septs:

ALLAN	BUIE	MACILROY	SUTTIE
BISSET	GILROY	MACKERRON	
BISSETT	MACALLAN	MACKIARAN	
BOWIE	MACGILROY	PRATT	

GUNN (Map H2) Though largely a Pictish tribe, the name probably equivalent to the Welsh 'Gwynn', the clan Gunn chiefs claimed Norse descent from one Gunni, son of a 12th-century Orcadian Olaf, acquiring Caithness lands from his mother's side, the Earls of Ross. A turbulent clan much in feud with the Keiths and MacKays, they found it advisable in the 15th century to move from Caithness to the Kildonan district of Sutherland. The sept names derive mostly from chief's sons as Johnson, MacIan, Mackean, Kean, Keene, all from 'son of John'. James (or Hamish), John, Henry (Eanrick), Rob and Will were all sons of the same 14th-century George Gunn, the 'Crowner' (royal legal deputy), William, of a later chief.

Septs:

ENRICK	KEAN	MACOMISH	ROBSON
GALDIE	KEENE	MACROB	SANDISON
GALLIE	MACCOMAS	MACWILLIAM	SWAN
GANSON	MACCORKILL	MAGNUS	SWANN
GAULDIE	MACCORKLE	MAIN	SWANNEY
GAUNSON	MACCULLIE	MANN	SWANSON
GEORGESON	MACIAN	MANSON	WILL
HENDERSON	MACKAMES	MANUS	WILLIAMSON
INRIG	MACKEAMISH	NEILSON	WILLS
JAMESON	MACKEAN	NELSON	WILSON
JAMIESON	MACMAINS	ROBINSON	WYLIE
JOHNSON	MACMANUS	ROBISON	WYLLIE

HAY (Map I6, K4) Hays have held ranks in France and elsewhere from early times. Several accompanied William the Conqueror in 1066; and a century later a descendant from these, William de la Haya, appears as cup-bearer to Malcolm IV and progenitor of the many branches of the Scottish clan. His elder son, William, became ancestor to the Earls of Errol; his younger, Robert, to the Yester branch and Marquises of Tweeddale. After Bannockburn, Bruce awarded Sir Gilbert Hay of Errol the Aberdeenshire lands of Slains and the hereditary High Constableship of Scotland.

Septs: CONSTABLE   GIFFORD   MACKESTER

HOME (Map K7) The name, properly pronounced 'Hume' and frequently so spelt, comes from the lands in Berwickshire acquired in marriage by a 13th-century descendant of the Northumbrian Earl Gospatrick, ancestor also of the Dunbars. By further marriages the Homes extended widely over the east Borderland and took full share in its wars and forays. David Hume (1711-76), philosopher-historian and indirect inspirer of many efforts to bring logic into practical history, also John Home, minister unfrocked for producing his poetic drama *Douglas* in 1756, might both claim family predecessors. Lord Kames, the lawyer-philosopher, and Lady Grizel Baillie, the balladist, were likewise born of the clan sometimes named 'the Haughty Homes'.

Septs:

AYTON	EATON	LANDELS	WEDDERBURN
BUNCLE	GREENLAW	MACK	
BUNKLE	HALIBURTON	NESBITT	
DUNBAR	LANDALE	NISBET	

INNES (Map I3) The name is from Gaelic *Innis*, an inch or islet, being one near Elgin on lands granted to the Innes' ancestor Berowald in 1154 by Malcolm IV for service against the rebelling Moray tribes of that time. While later branches extended to other districts, all were noted for loyalty in the Stewart causes.

Septs: INCH   MACROB   REIDFURD

JOHNSTON (Map I8)   John, a 12th-century holder of Annandale lands under the Bruces, gave name to his citadel or 'toun', from which his son took the surname de Johnston or Johnstone, the spelling indicating no real difference, though the 'e' is less frequent in north than south. A turbulent Border clan — hardly 'the Gentle Johnstones' to their Maxwell and Douglas rivals — they were frequently appointed Wardens of the West March, hence their motto 'Aye Ready'. The Aberdeenshire branch was founded by a 14th-century Steven de Johnston, from the Annandale family, marrying a Garrioch heiress. Johnstones of Coll are properly MacIans from Ardnamurchan, whilst occasional others have had the name as hailing from Perth, otherwise St John's-toun.

Septs:

JOHNSTONE	MARCHBANKS	MARJORIBANKS	ROME

KEITH (Map K5, K4, K3)   In the time of David I, Hervey de Keith possessed half of the lands named Keith in southwest East Lothian, and his great-grandson acquired the other half by marrying its Fraser heiress. As hereditary Grand Marischals of Scotland, the chiefs took a prominent part in the country's affairs and battles, and attained vast possessions, principally northwards. About 1390, Sir William Keith was the builder of historic Dunottar Castle (Map K5) as his main seat; and in 1593 the fifth Earl Marischal founded the famous Marischal College of Aberdeen. The tenth and last Earl forfeited title and all estates for active support of the Old Chevalier in 1715. The numerous Dicksons of the Border and Dixons in England descend from one of the early Keiths-Marischal.

Septs:

AUSTIN	DIXSON	HERVEY	MARSHALL
DICKISON	FALCONER	HURRIE	URIE
DICKSON	HARVEY	HURRY	URRY
DIXON	HAXTON	LUMGAIR	

KENNEDY (Map F8)   A genealogist has suggested the name to mean 'a kinsman', Henry Cinnidh or Kennedy being a younger brother of William the Lion and founder of this great Carrick clan. From supporting Bruce against the Comyns and James II against the Black Douglases, the Kennedies acquired great power in the land, albeit rocked by a centuries-long feud for seniority between the Bargany and Cassillis branches. One chief, the Earl of Cassillis in Mary's reign (and fighter in her cause), even ventured on the unofficial title 'King of Carrick'. Branches spread into Lennox in the 13th century, and Aberdeenshire in the 14th. The learned Bishop James Kennedy (and his daughter Kate) are still celebrated annually by the students of St Andrews University, where he founded a college in 1455.

Septs:

CARRICK	CASSELS	CASSILLIS	MACWALRICK

KERR (Map K7)   The Scottish Kers, Cars or Kerrs are recorded in Border history from the 12th century, after Normans of the name had been established in England from the Conquest. Though with offshoots reaching Ayrshire and Aberdeen by the 13th century, their main ground was Roxburghshire. There the Kerrs were early Sheriffs, and the principal divisions of the family became Kers of Cessford, of whom the Duke of Roxburgh is now chief, and Kerrs of Ferniehirst, now represented by the Marquess of Lothian.

Septs:

CARR	CARRE	CESSFORD	KER

LAMONT (Map E7)   The Clan MacEarcher (i.e. from some Farquhar chief, earlier than the northern Farquharsons' ancestor) were the immemorial of their part of Argyllshire, centred on Castle Toward in Cowal. A chief or his son in the 13th century seemingly acquired a special judicial rank that earned the clan, or its earliest branch, the new name 'Law-man', hence Laumon, Lamont and other variations. The clan lost power and territory to Campbells and other neighbours through marriages and less gentle means. A Dunoon monument recalls the 1646 capture and destruction of Toward Castle, with the subsequent massacre of many principal Lamonts on the excuse of their adherence to the royalist cause. The chief's seat thereafter became Ardlamont, at the other end of the Kyles of Bute.

Septs:

BLACK	LAMOND	MACERCHAR	MACMUNN
BLACKIE	LAMONDSON	MACERRACHER	MACPATRICK
BLAIK	LEMMON	MACFARQUHAR	MACPHUN
BLAIKIE	LEMOND	MACGILLEDOW	MACSORLEY
BLAKE	LIMOND	MACGORRIE	MEIKLEHAM
BROUN	LIMONT	MACILDOWIE	MEIKLEM
BROWN	LUCAS	MACILWHOM	MUNN
BURDEN	LUCK	MACKERCHAR	PATERSON
BURDON	LUCKIE	MACKERRACHER	PATRICK
CLEMENT	LUKE	MACLAMOND	SORLEY
DOUGLAS	MACALDOWIE	MACLEMON	TOWARD
FORSYTH	MACALDUIE	MACLUCAS	TOWART
LAMB	MACCLEMENT	MACLUCKIE	TURNER
LAMBIE	MACCLYMONT	MACLUKE	WHITE
LAMMIE	MACEARACHER	MACLYMONT	WHYTE

LESLIE (Map J4, I3)   The name is from the lands of Leslie in Garrioch, Aberdeenshire, granted to Malcolm, son of Bartholf or Bartholomew, under King William the Lion. A 13th-century descendant obtained grant of the Fife lands now also called Leslie; and a later marriage brought to the family the earldom of Rothes in Moray, now seat of the chief. John Leslie (1526-96), Bishop of Ross, was a notable historian and devoted champion to Mary Queen of Scots. Then in the following century there were at one time active three Generals Leslie: Walter, Count Leslie, with the German Emperor, whilst Alexander and David Leslie both earned distinction first with Gustavus Adolphus, then with Scotland's Covenanting armies.

Septs: ABERNETHY   LESSLIE   MORE

LINDSAY (Map J5–J7)   The widespread Lindsays claim Norman origin, the name from an 'Isle of lime-trees' near Rouen and said to have been spelt nearly 200 different ways, as Limesay, Lindesey etc. in England. Under David I, Sir Walter Lindsay was the first to hold position in Scotland, the family settling by Tweedside, from Earlston to Caddonlea. Connected from the 12th century with Crawford on Upper Clyde (hence their chief earldom title), by the 14th they had extended by marriage to Fife and Angus. 'The Lindsays light and gay' — and some who were neither — took high rank in Scotland's affairs and battles. Sir David Lindsay of the Mount, tutor to King James V, could infuse gaiety into the reforming courage of his great drama of 1540, *The Three Estates*. The Lord Lindsay of 1740 was the first Colonel of the Black Watch regiment.

Septs:

BUYERS	CRAWFORD	DOWNIE	RHYND
BYERS	DEUCHAR	FOTHERINGHAM	SUMMERS
COBB	DEUCHARS	RHIND	SUMNER

MACALISTER (Map D7)   The ancestor to this earliest offshoot from the great Clan Donald was Allister (or Alexander), eldest son of Angus, Lord of the Isles and Kintyre. Through joining the MacDougalls against Robert Bruce, Alister forfeited his succession to that lordship, but his descendants, inhabiting a tract of Knapdale and North Kintyre, grew strong enough to extend into Arran and Bute and became an independent clan when the Lords of the Isles were suppressed in 1493. Their first Knapdale stronghold of Castle Sweyn was assaulted by Bruce, whereafter the chief's seat became Ardpatrick, and finally Loup in Kintyre. Though having lost much of its territory and strength to the Campbells, the clan appeared in the royalist ranks with Montrose, and again at Killiecrankie.

Septs:

ALASTAIR	ALLISON	MACALLISTER
ALEXANDER	ALLISTER	SANDERS
ALISON	MACALASTER	SAUNDERS

MACARTHUR (Map F6)   This early branch of the Campbell clan long claimed its chiefship. The Argyllshire MacArthurs of Bruce's time took their part against the MacDougalls of Lorne and were richly rewarded out of the latter's territory, including the custodianship of Dunstaffnage Castle. Their own too-ambitious power was broken in 1427 when John MacArthur, their chief, forfeited to King James I all clan territory and his own head to the block. The clan afterwards acquired footings at Strachur in Cowal and around Glendochart, whilst a sept of them were hereditary pipers to the MacDonalds of the Isles.

Septs:

ARTHUR	CAMPBELL	MACCAIRTER	MACINDEOR
ARTHURSON	DEWAR	MACCARTER	

MACAULAY (Map F7, B2)   The Dunbartonshire Macaulays claim descent from MacGregor and hence MacAlpin stock. Seated at Ardincaple (now Helensburgh) since at least the 13th century, they were under protection of and closely connected with the old Earls of Lennox. It is from a brother, Aulay, of the Earl in Alexander II's time that the clan name is believed to derive. A branch that removed to Loch Fyne took the name MacPhedran, which became Paterson.

Lord Macaulay (1800-59), writer and statesman but famed chiefly for his *History of England*, was descended of a different small clan that was settled at Uig, on the west side of the Isle of Lewis. Of Norse origin, the name here deriving from 'Olaf', these Northern Macaulays were often at feud with the neighbouring Morrisons and usurping MacKenzies.

Septs of the Lennox clan:

MACALL	MACKELL	MACPHEIDRAN
MACCALL	MACPHEDRAN	PATERSON
MACKAIL	MACPHEDRON	PATTERSON

Septs of either clan:

	AULAY	MACAULLY
	MACALLEY	MACCAULEY

MACBEAN (Map I4)   This clan in Moray was one of the Clan Chattan confederacy. Although in the 'Forty-five' they served with gallantry under Lochiel, normally they followed the Macintosh banner, their founder having arrived in the suite of the 1291 MacPherson heiress who married the Macintosh chief. Originally they claim common stock with the Macbeths, from that 11th-century king of Scotland.

Septs:

BEAN	MACBEATH	MACILVEEN	MACVEAN
BINNIE	MACBETH	MACVAIN	
MACBAIN	MACILVAIN	MACVANE	

C

MACBETH (Map I3) One of the exceptions among the 'Macs', the name means not the son of any person 'Beth', but 'Son of life', or a man of religion. It developed a separate form Macbean (see above), and has also become confused with forms of the Norman name Bethune. Shakespeare, playing his immortal light over the old Celtic throne of Scotland, brings to focus the ruler of Moray who enforced his family claim thereon by the murder of King Duncan in 1040. Macbeths, frequently called Beatons, held high repute and rank from the 14th century to the 17th, as physicians and chancellors to the MacDonalds of Islay and Macleans of Mull, sometimes also to royalty and elsewhere.

Septs:

BEATON	BEATTY	BETHUNE	MACBHEATH
BEATTIE	BELTON	LEITCH	MACBHEATH

MACDONALD (of the Isles):
CLAN DONALD NORTH (Map C3, D4, A3)
CLAN DONALD SOUTH (Map D7, C7)
Greatest and most widespread of all, Clan Donald has its main roots in the old Gaelic and Pictish times, with additions from the Norsemen just when the curtain of history begins lifting on personalities. There is a legendary ancestor, Conn of the Battles, but the first clear one is Somerled, the thane of Argyll who became wellnigh an independent king of the 'South Isles' (from Ardnamurchan round to Bute), swaying his naval alliance between the rival powers of Scotland and Norway. In 1135 he helped David I expel the Norse from Arran and Bute, and eventually fell at Renfrew in 1164 when himself invading against Malcolm IV. Of his three sons by a daughter of Olaf, Norse king of the Isle of Man, the eldest founded the MacDougall clan of Lorne, and the next son, Reginald or Ranald, was ancestor to all the clans that derive name from his eldest son, Donald. The descendants of Donald's eldest son, Angus Mor mac Donald, formed Clan Donald South, centred on Islay. Those of the second son, Roderick or Rorie, were granted the isles north of Ardnamurchan after Haakon's defeat at Largs (Map F7) and the confinement after 1266 of the Norse to Orkney and Shetland only.

MacDonald allegiance to the Scottish crown was now unquestionable — so far as it could be induced or enforced. Bruce at Bannockburn granted the clan their jealously upheld honour of position on the right of the Scottish battle array; and in the following reign Angus Mor's grandson, John of Islay, reunited the North and South Isles by marrying the MacRorie heiress, and first assumed the Lordship of the Isles that needed royal suppression in 1493. The curbing royal policy likewise directed partitions into the separate branch-clans that follow. After 1493 the vast power of the Lords of the Isles was transferred to the Earls of Argyll in the South Isles and Huntly in the North Isles and Highlands, not without flaring resistances and memories that still cling. Chiefship shifted to the Sleat branch in Skye, called MacDonalds of the Isles to distinguish them from the branch-clans.

The numerous sept names have most various origins. Donaldson, MacConnell, Daniels, etc., are just variations from MacDonald. MacGorrie and MacHutcheon, otherwise MacQuistan, are examples of branches from chiefs Godfrey and Hugh. Small clans or families sought or fell under the MacDonald protection, or like the Macbeths took high service with the chiefs. Sometimes they took the MacDonald name irrespective of any descent from Somerled, sometimes retained their own or acquired new ones, like MacGowan (the smith's son) and Galt or Gaul (the stranger). Then when the refractory Clan Donald South was supposedly expelled from Kintyre and Islay, a strange crop of new names blossomed as in similar circumstances with the MacGregors and Lamonts.

Apart from the various strands of the MacDonald family mentioned below, two of the septs of the mighty Clan Donald, Darroch and MacSporran, have more recently been recognised by Lord Lyon King of Arms as separate, if small, clans in their own right.

Septs:

ALASTAIR	GORRY	MACCRORIE	MACMURCHIE
ALLISTER	GOWAN	MACCRUM	MACMURCHY
ANDERSON	GOWANS	MACCUAIG	MACMURDO
BALLACH	HAWTHORN	MACCUISH	MACMURDOCH
BALLOCH	HERON	MACCUITHEIN	MACO'SHANNAIG
BEATH	HEWISON	MACCUTCHEN	MACQUILKAN
BEATON	HOUSTOUN	MACCUTCHEON	MACQUISTAN
BETHUNE	HOUSTON	MACDANIELL	MACQUISTEN
BOWIE	HOWAT	MACDRAIN	MACRAITH
BRODIE	HOWE	MACEACHERN	MACREARIE
BUDGE	HOWIE	MACEACHRAN	MACRORIE
BUIE	HOWISON	MACELFRISH	MACRORY
BULLOCH	HUDSON	MACELHERAN	MACRUER
CAMBRIDGE	HUTCHEON	MACGAA	MACRURY
CATHAL	HUTCHESON	MACGAW	MACRYRIE
CATHIL	HUTCHIN	MACGEACHY	MACSORLEY
COCHRAN	HUTCHINSON	MACGECHIE	MACSPORRAN
COCHRANE	HUTCHISON	MACGEE	MACSWAN
COLL	HUTCHON	MACGHEE	MACSWEEN
COLSON	HUTSON	MACGHIE	MACWHAN
CONN	ISLES	MACGILL	MACWHANNELL
CONNAL	JEFFREY	MACGORRIE	MARK
CONNELL	KEEGAN	MACGORRY	MARQUIS
COOK	KEIGHREN	MACGOUN	MARTIN
COOKE	KELLY	MACGOW	MAY
COULL	KINNELL	MACGOWAN	MURCHIE
COULSON	LAING	MACGOWN	MURCHISON
CRIRIE	LANG	MACGRAIN	MURDOCH
CROMB	LEITCH	MACHUGH	MURDOSON
CROMBIE	MACARTHUR	MACHUTCHEN	MURPHY
CROOM	MACBEATH	MACHUTCHEON	O'MAY
CRUM	MACBETH	MACILLRICK	PATON
DANIEL	MACBHEATH	MACILREACH	PATTEN
DANIELS	MACBRAYNE	MACILREVIE	PEDEN
DARRACH	MACBRIDE	MACILRIACH	PURCELL
DARROCH	MACBRYDE	MACILWRAITH	REOCH
DONALD	MACCAA	MACILWRICK	REVIE
DONALDSON	MACCAIRN	MACKAY	RIACH
DONNELL	MACCAMBRIDGE	MACKEACHIE	RODERICK
DRAIN	MACCARRON	MACKEE	RORIE
DUNNEL	MACCAW	MACKEITHAN	RORISON
FORREST	MACCAY	MACKELLAIG	RYRIE
FORRESTER	MACCLUSKIE	MACKELLOCH	SHANNON
GALBRAITH	MACCODRUM	MACKERRON	SHENNAN
GALBREATH	MACCOLL	MACKEY	SORLEY
GALL	MACCONNAL	MACKIE	SORLIE
GALT	MACCONNELL	MACKIGGAN	SPORRAN
GAULD	MACCOOISH	MACKINNELL	TRAIN
GAUL	MACCOOK	MACLAIRISH	WHANNEL
GAULT	MACCOSHAM	MACLARDY	WHEELAN
GILBRIDE	MACCRAIN	MACLARTY	WHELLAN
GILL	MACCRAN	MACLAVERTY	WILKIE
GORRIE	MACCRIRIE	MACLEVERTY	WILKINSON

MACDONALD of Ardnamurchan (Map C5)

The MacDonalds or MacIans of Ardnamurchan were founded there, in Robert Bruce's time, by Ian, a son of Angus Mor mac Donald above mentioned. In 1495 they were hosts at Mingary to James IV and assisted him against rebellious chiefs. But early in the 17th century they suffered persecution with the rest of Clan Donald South, and a number of the clan having been goaded into an act of piracy, this was unjustly remembered against their innocent Glencoe namesakes in 1692. The following are all variations from the clan name MacIan:

Septs:

JOHNSON	KEENE	MACKAIN	MACKEAN
JOHNSTONE	MACIAN	MACKANE	MACKEAND
KEAN			

MACDONALD of Clanranald (Map D5, C5, A4)

Strictly, all the MacDonald clans are of Clan Ranald and were frequently so termed, from Donald's father, Reginald or Ranald. Thus some confusion arises when a particular branch-clan adopts that general name, instead of their more correct form MacRanald. They derive from another Ranald, doubly descended from the first, being a younger son of John, first Lord of the Isles, by the MacRorie heiress whom he afterwards unjustly divorced. The elder son, Godfrey, claimed the North Isles inheritance in his own right, but was rejected in favour of Ranald who, being agreeable to his father's dubious superiority, was presented with the North Isles along with a thriving nest of feuds for his descendants. The clan established their position in the island-chain Benbecula to Eigg, also in their other grant from John, that rugged mainland tract from Moidart to Knoydart that Prince Charlie came to know so intimately among the faithful Clanranald.

Septs:

ALCOCK	KETCHEN	MACEACHAN	MACKESSICK
ALISON	KETCHIN	MACEACHEN	MACKICHAN
ALLAN	MACACHIN	MACEACHIN	MACKISSOCK
ALLANSON	MACAICHAN	MACGACHAN	MACMURRAY
ALLEN	MACALLAN	MACGEACHAN	MACMURRICH
CALLAN	MACBURIE	MACISAAC	MACVARISH
CALLEN	MACCRINDLE	MACKEACHAN	MACVURICH
CURRIE	MACCURRACH	MACKECHNIE	MACVURIE
ISAAC	MACCURRIE	MACKEOCHAN	MACVURRICH
ISAACS	MACDONALD	MACKESSACK	PARK

MACDONALD of Glencoe (Map E5)

This small branch-clan descends from Ian Og, i.e. 'young John', grandson of Angus Mor (see MacDonald) and step-brother to the first Lord of the Isles who, in the 14th century, settled Ian on the land having that rugged defile Glencoe, traditional birthplace of a Gaelic Homer, Ossian. These MacIans or MacDonalds lived there peaceably until the notorious 1692 massacre (Map F5), when governmental spite against all sympathisers with the deposed Stewarts was vented so cold-bloodedly against a clan innocent of other offence.

Septs:

HENDERSON	KEAN	MACHENDRY	MACPHILIP
HENDRIE	KEENE	MACHENRY	PHILIP
HENDRY	MACDONALD	MACIAN	PHILP
HENRY	MACGILP	MACKEAN	
JOHNSON	MACHENDRIE	MACKILLOP	

MACDONELL of Glengarry (Map E4, F4, E3) The different spelling of MacDonald was adopted in the 17th century by this early division from the Clanranald branch. The Glengarry founder was Alister, second son of Donald, eldest son of the 14th-century Ranald. Apart from disputes of their own with the neighbouring MacKenzies, the Glengarries went along with the other Clanranalds, particularly in support of all the Stewart causes.

Septs:

ALASTAIR	COWAN	MACOWAN	SANDERSON
ALEXANDER	MACCOWAN	SANDER	SAUNDERS
ALLISTER	MACDONELL	SANDERS	

MACDONNELL of Keppoch (Map F5) The MacDonalds or MacDonnells of Keppoch (the spelling altered also in the 17th century) descended from Alister Currach, third son of John, first Lord of the Isles (see MacDonald) by his second wife, a sister of King Robert II. From Alister's great-grandson, Ranald, the clan was also sometimes known as Clanranald of Lochaber. For centuries they occupied their territory by unwritten clan right, despite a feudal charter granted to the Macintoshes. In their support of the Stewarts, Ian Lom, celebrated also as a Gaelic bard, acted guide for Montrose's master-stroke, the surprise march on snowbound Inverlochy Castle in 1645. And in 'the forty-five' the Keppochs captured two government companies before Prince Charlie's banner was actually raised.

Septs:

MACDONELL	MACPHILIP	MICHIE	PHILP
MACGILLIVANTIC	MACRONALD	MICHIESON	RAINNIE
MACGILP	MECHIE	PHILIP	RENNIE
MACGLASRICH	MEEKISON	PHILIPSON	RONALD
MACKILLOP	MEKIE	PHILLIP	RONALDSON
MACMICHIE	MICHAEL	PHILLIPS	

MACDOUGALL (Map E6, E9) The MacDougalls of the Argyllshire district of Lorne trace back to the same ancestors as the MacDonalds, being named from the first Lord of Lorne, Dougall, the eldest son of Somerled by Ragnhildis, daughter of Olaf, the King of Man. But her mother, Alfrica, was already a McDougall or McDowall of the still older Galloway branch, Alfrica's father being Fergus Mac Dubh Gael, the powerful 12th-century Lord of Galloway and founder of several abbeys in that ancient Pictish-Celtic territory.

MacDougall history is mainly coloured by their feud with Robert Bruce after his hasty slaying of the Red Comyn, claimant to the Scottish throne (see Clan Cumming). Alexander, fourth Lord of Lorne, had married Comyn's sister. After Bruce's defeat at Methven by the English, he took for a time to the Grampians. At Dalree in Strathfillan his party was set upon by a strong force of MacDougalls, and Bruce himself escaped only by leaving his plaid grasped by a dying MacDougall. Attached to it was the magnificent Celtic 'Brooch of Lorne', still in the treasured possession of the clan chief at Dunollie. Eventually Bruce overcame both the English and the MacDougalls, the latter being restored to their Lorne lands only when Alexander's grandson, Ewen, married a niece of David II. By Ewen having only heiresses, the lordship of Lorne passed to Stewart hands, whilst the male branch of Dunollie retained the clan chiefship.

Septs:

CARMICHAEL	DOUGAL	DUGALD	LIVINGSTONE
COLES	DOUGALL	EUNSON	LUCAS
CONACHER	DOWALL	HOWELL	MACCLINTOCK
COWAN	DOWELL	HOWELLS	MACCONACHER
COWEN	DUGAL	LIVINGSTON	MACCONCHER

MACCOUL	MACDOOL	MACEWEN	MACLUGASH
MACCOWAN	MACDOUGAL	MACHALE	MACLULLICH
MACCOWELL	MACDOUL	MACHOWELL	MACNAMELL
MACCOYLE	MACDOWALL	MACKICHAN	MACOUAL
MACCULLAGH	MACDOWELL	MACLINDEN	MACOUL
MACCULLOCH	MACDUGALD	MACLINTOCK	MACOWAN
MACDILL	MACEWAN	MACLUCAS	MACOWEN

MACDUFF (Map I6, J3)   Like the clan's claim of descent from Clan Alpin, the real story of Shakespeare's Macduff overthrowing Macbeth in 1056 remains uncertain, but the hereditary special privileges and dispensations once known as 'Law Clan Macduff' must have originated from some other notable service. Thus, it was accepted even by Edward I, 'Hammer of the Scots', that a Scottish king could be properly crowned only by a Macduff. Edward retained that young chief at the English court and gave him his granddaughter's hand, but Macduff's sister Isabel, Countess of Buchan, crowned King Robert Bruce in 1306. Captured later by Edward, she was punished by confinement in a cage at Berwick.

Until among the first Earls created by David I, the Macduff Thanes of Fife held their territory in the old Celtic manner 'by grace of God', not from the King — hence occasional mentions of the county as though of itself a 'kingdom'. Their direct line failed with another 14th-century Isabel, but the Duff families then first heard of in Aberdeenshire claim to carry on the clan. They reacquired a title Earl, then Duke of Fife, but their territory remained around where they founded the fishing town Macduff.

Septs:

DUFF	FYFFE	SPENCE	WEMYSS
FIFE	HUME	SPENS	
FYFE	KILGOUR	WEEMS	

MACFARLANE (Map F6)   This clan of Loch-Lomondside and Arrochar descended from the old Celtic earls of Lennox through Gilchrist, younger brother of Malduin, a 13th-century Earl. The name derives from his great-grandson, Bartholomew or Parlan. From failures in the direct male line, the clan lands passed to other ownership by feudal law, while rightfully elective male chiefs were dispossessed. From this disorganisation and a feud with the powerful Colquhouns resulting in that Chief being slain in 1608, the clan were for a time outlawed like the MacGregors, or transferred elsewhere in Scotland or to Ireland. Many groups thereafter retained the various other names they adopted at the time, like the MacAllans in Aberdeenshire.

Septs:

ALLAN	KENNIESON	MACKINLAY	MUNNOCK
ALLANACH	LEAPER	MACNAIR	NAPIER
ALLANSON	LEIPPER	MACNEUR	PARLAN
ALLEN	LENNOX	MACNIDER	PARLANE
ALLISON	MACAINDRA	MACNITER	ROBB
BARTHOLOMEW	MACALLAN	MACNUIR	SMITH
BARTIE	MACCAUSE	MACPARLAND	SPREULL
BARTLEMAN	MACCONDACH	MACPARLANE	SPROUL
BARTLET	MACCONDY	MACPHARLAN	STALKER
BARTLETT	MACERRACHER	MACROB	THOMASON
BARTY	MACFARLAN	MACROBB	WEAVER
BRYCE	MACGEOCH	MACWALTER	WEBSTER
CALLANDER	MACGREUSICH	MACWILLIAM	WEIR
CUNNISON	MACGURK	MILLAR	WILLIAMSON
GALBRAITH	MACINALLY	MILLER	WYLIE
GALBREATH	MACINSTALKER	MONACH	WYLLIE
GALLOWAY	MACJAMES	MUNNOCH	

MACFIE (Map C6)   The MacFies claim to be one of the ancient Clan Alpin, and come no doubt from some dark-featured ancestor, as is signified by the earlier form MacDuffie; perhaps from the Dubhshith who in 1164 was lector at the cathedral on the sacred isle of Iona, where there is also a monument to a later McFie chief. Twenty miles south lies Colonsay, which was the clan's own island, with their burial-ground on neighbouring Oronsay. In the 17th century they were dispossessed and dispersed in various directions. The MacFie followers of Cameron of Lochiel earned particular tribute at Culloden.

Septs:

CATHIE	MACCATHIE	MACGUFFIE	MACVEE
DUFFIE	MACCOOISH	MACHAFFIE	MACVIE
DUFFY	MACCUISH	MACNICOL	
FEE	MACDUFFIE	MACPHEE	
MACCAFFIE	MACFEE	MACPHIE	

MACGILLIVRAY (Map D5, G4)   Originally an Argyllshire clan and one of the great MacDonald group, the MacGillivrays were involved in the latter's defeat in 1222 by Alexander II. Thereafter, a branch in Morvern came under protection of the MacLeans of Mull, but about 1263 the chief section removed to Macintosh country and joined Clan Chattan under that leadership. However, at Culloden with Prince Charlie it was their chief, MacGillivray of Dunmaglass, who most gallantly led the Macintoshes. The MacInnes branch of the Morvern MacGillivrays appear as a separate clan.

Septs:

GILRAY	MACGILROY	MACILROY	ROY
GILROY	MACGILVRA	MACILVRAE	
GILVRAY	MACGILVRAY	MILROY	

MACGREGOR (Map F6)   Recorded in Glen Orchy from about the 12th century and spreading to Glenstrae and several Perthshire glens, the MacGregors take their motto *Is Rioghal mo dhream,* 'My race is Royal', from a traditional ancestor, Gregor or Girig, of the ancient Clan Alpin dynasty. They held doggedly to the old Celtic clan rule of defending possession by the sword, in defiance of 'sheepskin' feudal charters obtained through marriage or more dubious means by powerful neighbours having a closer approach to the government's ear — notably the Campbells, Grahams and Colquhouns. After a defeat by these last at Glen Fruin in 1603, there came a long succession of vindictive edicts, fomenting and taking full excuse from the MacGregors' spirit of untamed resentment. The clan was outlawed, and a ban on using their surname not lifted until 1784 except in the time of the Stewart Restoration, in recognition of their loyal service with Montrose. From these prescriptions arose the many 'sept' names then adopted by scattered groups of MacGregors — also the remarkable career of Rob Roy and Scott's stirring song 'The MacGregors' Gathering'.

Septs:

ARGYL	CLARK	FISHER	GREIG
ARROWSMITH	COMRIE	FLETCHER	GREWAR
BARROWMAN	CRAIGDALLIE	GAIR	GREYSON
BEGLAND	CRERAR	GOODSIR	GRIER
BLACK	CROWTHER	GREER	GRIERSON
BOWER	DENNISON	GREGG	GRIGG
BOWMAKER	DENSON	GREGOR	GRIGOR
CAIRD	DOCHART	GREGORSON	GRUER
CALLENDAR	DOCHERTY	GREGORY	GUDGER
CALLUM	DOWIE	GREGSON	GUINNESS

Septs:

JOHNSTON	MACDOUGAL	MACNEICE	PATTULLO
KING	MACEWEN	MACNEISH	PEAT
KIRKWOOD	MACGEACH	MACNESS	PETER
LAIKIE	MACGREWAR	MACNEY	PETERS
LECKIE	MACGRIGOR	MACNIE	PETERSON
LECKY	MACGROUTHER	MACNIESH	PETRIE
MACADAM	MACGRUDER	MACNISH	ROBINS
MACAINSH	MACGRUER	MACNOCAIRD	ROY
MACALDOWIE	MACGRUMEN	MACNUCATOR	SKINNER
MACALESTER	MACGRUTHER	MACONACHIE	STALKER
MACANGUS	MACIAN	MACPETER	STIRLING
MACANISH	MACILDOWIE	MACPETRIE	STRINGER
MACARA	MACILDUFF	MACWILLIAM	TAINSH
MACAREE	MACILDUY	MAGREW	TOSSACK
MACCAINSH	MACINNES	MALLOCH	WALKER
MACCANCE	MACINSTALKER	NEISH	WELIVER
MACCANSH	MACINTYRE	NELSON	WHITE
MACCONACHIE	MACLEISTER	NICE	WHYTE
MACCONDACH	MACLIVER	NISH	WILCOX
MACCONDOCHIE	MACNAY	NUCATOR	WILLOX
MACCROUTHER	MACNEA	ORR	
MACCRUITER	MACNEE	PATERSON	

MACINNES (Map D5)   The name Innes here comes from the Gaelic pronunciation of MacAngus. A Morvern branch of the Clan MacGillivray, the MacInneses were for long Constables of the important fortress of Kinlochaline on the Sound of Mull. MacInneses are also recorded as hereditary instructors in archery to the Clan MacKinnon. The MacMasters were originally a separate clan of neighbouring Ardgour, driven from there by MacLeans in the 14th century.

Angus being an ancient and favourite Scottish forename, MacInnes and its variants sprang up independently of the above clan, as in Galloway and notably in Perthshire, where the MacNish or MacCance septs are attributed to MacGregor origin.

Septs:

ANGUS	MACANISH	MACCANSH
MACAINSH	MACCAINSH	MACMASTER
MACANGUS	MACCANCE	MASTERSON

MACINTOSH (Map G4, H5)   This leading division of the old Clan Chattan claims the Macintoshes descended from Seach or Shaw, son of a Macduff thane of Fife. Assisting Malcolm IV about 1160 to quell a rebel rising in Moray, he was awarded lands near Inverness and the constableship of that castle. The name means 'Son of the Toisich' or 'Toshach', i.e. of the leader or general. The clan occupied an important central position but in clashes with neighbours like the ambitious Gordons managed well to maintain itself, through astute compromise between the two types of Scottish feudalism. Though in many ways adhering to the old Celtic clan system, their actual power was based on royal charters and a female inheritance. In the last of their successive rallies for the Stewarts, the clan was raised for Prince Charlie by Lady Macintosh, despite the neutrality of her husband, the Chief. Placed under command of a MacGillivray, they were the first to charge at Culloden.

The clan chief, Mackintosh of Mackintosh, retains a superfluous English 'k' in the name. The MacThomas or MacTavish septs, settled in Glenshee or West Angus, derive from a son of a 14th-century Macintosh chief, whilst the Farquharson and Shaw branches are regarded as having become separate clans. The MacThomas sept has also recently become a separate clan.

Septs:

ADAMSON	HARDY	MACCOMIE	MACRITCHIE
AYSON	HEGGIE	MACCONCHIE	MACTAUSE
CASH	HIGGISON	MACFAIL	MACTAVISH
CLARK	HOSICK	MACFALL	MACTHOMAS
CLARKE	HOSSACK	MACFAULD	MACVAIL
CLARKSON	LEARY	MACGLASHAN	NAIRN
CLERK	MACANDREW	MACGLASHEN	NAIRNE
COMBE	MACARTNEY	MACHARDIE	NEVISON
COMBIE	MACAY	MACHARDY	NIVEN
CREARER	MACCAISH	MACKEGGIE	NOBLE
CRERAR	MACCARDNEY	MACKIESON	PAUL
DALLAS	MACCARTNEY	MACKILLICAN	RIPLEY
DOLES	MACCASH	MACKINTOSH	RITCHIE
EASON	MACCAUSE	MACLEAR	SIVEWRIGHT
EASSON	MACCHLERY	MACLEARY	TARRELL
EGGIE	MACCLAIR	MACLEHOSE	TAWESON
EGGO	MACCLEARY	MACLERIE	TAWSE
ELDER	MACCOLM	MACNEVIN	THOM
ESSON	MACCOMAS	MACNIVEN	THOMS
GLENNIE	MACCOMBE	MACOMIE	TOSH
GLENNY	MACCOMBICH	MACOMISH	TOSHACH
HARDIE	MACCOMBIE	MACPHAIL	

MACINTYRE (Map E6)   By tradition a branch from the Skye MacDonalds, the clan achieved most note from their bards and musicians. The name means 'Son of the wright' or 'carpenter'. For centuries, until 1810, inhabiting Glen Noe off Loch Etive, the MacIntyres were too small to stand alone and first followed the banner of the Appin Stewarts then latterly of the Campbell superiors of their land, though one branch became hereditary pipers to the Menzies chiefs.

Septs:

MACCOSHAM	MACKINTYRE	MACTIER	TYRE
MACINTIRE	MACTEAR	MACTIRE	WRIGHT

MACKAY (Map F2)   Like their MacKenzie neighbours, the MacKays of the Cape Wrath district, sometimes termed Clan Morgan after a 14th-century chief, may have been one of the tribes of Moray expelled from there for revolts in the 12th century. This powerful clan came often into dispute with others, not excluding the great Lords of the Isles. A strong section of the clan became established under these lords in Argyll and Galloway, and the name MacKay derives from Morgan's grandson Aodh, whose mother was a MacNeil of Gigha. MacKays or MacAys of Clan Chattan, from Inverness-shire eastward, are really of Clan MacDhai, i.e., Davidsons.

Clan MacKay devoted much zeal to the Protestant Reformation. Two thousand of them crossed the North Sea to serve that cause in the Thirty-Years' War. Charles I raised their Chief to Lord Dreay, yet their grandsons' religious mistrust of the Stewarts made them one of the anti-Jacobite clans.

Septs:

ALLAN	MACALLAN	MACGAA	MACKEE
BAIN	MACBAIN	MACGAW	MACKIE
BAYNE	MACCAA	MACGEE	MACPHAIL
KAY	MACCAW	MACGHEE	MACQUE
KEY	MACCAY	MACGHIE	MACQUEY

Septs:

MACQUOID	MORGAN	POLE	SCOBIE
MACVAIL	NEILSON	POLESON	WILLIAMSON
MACVAIN	NELSON	POLSON	
MACVANE	PAUL	REAY	

MACKENZIE (Map F3, D3)   Perhaps, like the MacKays and MacLeans, one of the old transplanted tribes from Moray, though firmly rooted in Ross-shire ever since, this clan took their name, MacKenny or MacKenzie, after a 13th-century chief Kenneth, descended from Colin of the Aird who was ancestor also to the Celtic Earls of Ross. When that earldom fell by marriage to the Lord of the Isles, the clan followed the MacDonald lead until these lords were suppressed. Independence attained, the MacKenzies became by the 17th century the most powerful clan of the West after the Campbells, and their chief, MacKenzie of Kintail, was raised to Lord Seaforth by James VI. This earldom was forfeited through the clans sharing the Jacobite ventures but restored in 1778 when the Seaforth Highlanders regiment was founded.

Septs:

CHARLES	KENNETH	MACKENNA	MACVINISH
CHARLESON	KENNETHSON	MACKENNEY	MACVINNIE
CLUNESS	KYNOCH	MACKERLICH	MACWEENY
CLUNIES	MACAWEENEY	MACKINNEY	MACWHINNIE
CROMARTY	MACBEOLAIN	MACMURCHIE	MURCHIE
IVERACH	MACCONNACH	MACMURCHY	MURCHISON
IVERSON	MACIVER	MACQUEENIE	SMART
IVORY	MACIVOR	MACVANISH	

MACKINNON (Map D4, E7)   By old tradition the MacKinnons claim to be of the royal Clan Alpin stock, descended and named from Fingon, brother to Andrew who was ancestor to Grigor and the MacGregors. From actual records we find them from about 1400 established as vassals of the Lords of the Isles in East Skye, including Castles Strathardle and Maol, and in Mull, with branches from Tiree to Arran. Like the other Alpin branch MacFie, they had at least a professional interest in the holy isle of Iona, where several MacFingons or MacKinnons were abbots around the 15th century.

The clan 'came out' with Montrose and in both Jacobite rebellions. In July 1746 the aged Chief and his family took over from Flora MacDonald a further anxious stage in aiding Prince Charlie's escape after Culloden.

Septs:

LOVE	MACKINNING	MACMORRAN	SHERRIE
MACINNON	MACKINVEN	MACSHERRIE	SHERRY

MACLACHLAN (Map E6)   From time immemorial the clan home has been Strathlachlan on the Cowal side of Loch Fyne, beside their neighbours, the MacEwens and Lamonts. Ancient tradition has it the three were originally founded by brothers, and these related by marraige, if not descent, to the ancient Kings of Ireland and Somerled Lords of the Isles. Their name may derive from that founder Lachlan, or from the O Loughlins, or from a later chief, Lachlan Mor of the 13th century. A section of the clan acquired Loch Awe territory under Campbell leadership, and another similarly served with the Lochiel Camerons.

The MacEwan group of septs might fairly claim separate clanship; whilst those of them in Lorne and Breadalbane are attributed to a MacDougall origin.

Septs:

EUNSON	EWEN	EWING	LACHIE
EWAN	EWENSON	GILCHRIST	LACHLAN

Septs:

LAUCHLAN	MACEWEN	MACKEWAN	MACLAGHLAN
MACCUNE	MACGILCHRIST	MACKEWN	MACLAUCHLAN
MACOUNN	MACKEON	MACKUEN	MACLAUGHLIN
MACEWAN	MACKEOWN	MACKUNE	

MACLAINE of Lochbuie See MACLEAN.

MACLAREN (Map G6) The older form MacLaurin is nearer to the Gaelic pronunciation. Whether originally called after the martyred St Lawrence, or from Loarn, son of the Erc who founded Scottish Dalriada about 503, and namer of the district of Lorne, the clan does claim descent from three brothers from the area now Argyll, who served with Kenneth MacAlpin in his successful campaign of 843-50 to unite the Northern Picts into Scotland. A branch remained in their first home-country and was for long in possession of Tiree, but those three brothers' awards in Balquhidder and Strathearn became the clan's main territory. Here they enter records surviving from the 13th century, and at Balquhidder lies Rob Roy MacGregor in the MacLaurin burial-ground: not the only old encroachment between these two clans. In their long record of loyalty the MacLaurins frequently followed the Appin Stewarts, with whom they had blood ties, and it was a MacLaurin who escaped Cumberland's troops by flinging himself over the Moffat 'Beef-tub'.

Septs:

FAED	LOWSON	MACLAURIN	PATTERSON
LARNACH	MACFADE	MACPATRICK	PETERKIN
LAURENCE	MACCLARENCE	MACPETRIE	PETERS
LAURENSON	MACCRORIE	MACPHAIT	PETERSON
LAW	MACFAIT	MACPHATER	RORIE
LAWRENCE	MACFATER	MACRORIE	RORISON
LAWSON	MACFEAD	MACRORY	
LOW	MACFEAT	PATERSON	
LOWE	MACGRORY	PATRICK	

MACLEAN (Map D6, B5, C5, E5) Though the name means 'Son of a devotee of St John', MacLeans claim as legendary ancestor a 5th-century Gillean-na Tuaidhe, i.e. Gillean of the Battle-axe. They may have been transplanted by Malcolm IV from Glen Urquhart, as one of the Celtic tribes then rebelling against centralised feudalism. A century later, the 13th, we find them in Mull, strongly established as vassals of Clan Donald, and soon one of the most powerful clans behind the Lords of the Isles, as at Harlaw 1411 and until these lords' suppression in 1493 and an ensuing feud with the MacDonalds that lasted till 1498. Their territory ranged from Coll and Tiree to Ardgour on the mainland, though the main families remained MacLeans of Duart (Chief) and Maclaines of Lochbuie, both in Mull. Their Chief fell protecting James IV at Flodden, and with their maxim the MacLeans must never turn their backs to a foe, the clan were prominent in all the Stewart causes.

Septs:

BEATH	MACBAY	MACFETRIDGE	MACVAY
BEATON	MACBEATH	MACGILLIVRAY	MACVEAGH
BEY	MACBETH	MACGILVRA	MACVEY
BLACK	MACBEY	MACILDOWIE	PADON
GILLAN	MACBHEATH	MACILDUFF	PATON
GILLAND	MACCLANE	MACILDUY	PATTEN
GILLIAN	MACCLEAN	MACILVORA	PATTON
GILLON	MACCORMICK	MACLAINE	PEDEN
GILZEAN	MACFADYEN	MACLERGAN	RANKEN
HUIE	MACFADZEAN	MACPHADDEN	RANKINE
LEAN	MACFAYDEN	MACRANKIN	

MACLENNAN (Map E4)   The small MacLennan clan of Kintail originated from a southern Logan marrying a Fraser and forming a Logan clan, at first in Easter Ross. Their 13th-century chief, Gilliegorm, then falling into strife with the Frasers, was killed and his widow imprisoned. Her posthumous son was deformed, whether by nature or by the gaolers, and delivered to the Beauly monks for a priestly education. He did found churches at Kilmor in Skye and Kilchrennan in Glenelg, but he also carried his clan, along with the closely associated Macraes, across to Kintail on the west coast, where he married and named his son Gille Fhinnan, after the Celtic St Finnan. From MacGill'innan comes 'MacLennan'. Sections of the clan later attached themselves to the Frasers and MacKenzies.

Septs:

LOBBAN	LOGAN

MACLEOD of Harris (Map B3, C4, E4)   The MacLeod chiefs claim descent from Leod, nephew of Magnus, the 13th-century last of the Norse kings of the Isle of Man; and from Leod's two sons, Tormod and Torquil, come respectively the Harris and Lewis branches. The bulk of the clan, however, remains of native Celtic stock. Tormod's grandson Malcolm was awarded a charter of Glenelg territory by David II and by marriage acquired the clan's large foothold in Skye, with its famed fortress of Dunvegan as the Chief's seat. Harris was held by MacLeods as vassals to Clan Donald until the Lords of the Isles were forfeited. Thereafter, clear of that entanglement, they aided the MacLeans against the MacDonalds. At Worcester in 1651, the clan lost so many men for Charles II that the other clans agreed to exonerate them from further conflicts.

Septs:

BEATON	HARROLD	MACCUAIG	NORMAN
BETHUNE	MACANDIE	MACHAROLD	NORMAND
BETON	MACCAIG	MACLURE	WILLIAMSON
GRIMMOND	MACCLURE	MACRAILD	
HAROLD	MACCRIMMON	MACWILLIAM	

MACLEOD of Lewis (Map C2, C4, D3, D4)   The clan of Torquil (see above) early became so powerful as to dispute the superiority of the Harris branch chiefship, attaining at least an independent status. Important branches were the MacGillechallum or MacLeods of Raasay, and those of Assynt. The MacNicols (Nicolson etc.) were originally an independent clan of the Assynt district (Map E2). They moved to the Portree corner of Skye after a 14th-century Lewis MacLeod had married their Chief's heiress.

Septs:

ASKEY	MACASKILL	MACCORQUODALE	NICHOLSON
AULAY	MACCABE	MACGILLECHALLUM	NICOL
CALLAM	MACAULAY	MACKASKILL	NICOLL
CALLUM	MACCALLUM	MACLEWIS	NICOLSON
CASKEY	MACCASKIE	MACNICHOL	NORIE
CASKIE	MACCASKILL	MACNICOL	NORRIE
LEWIS	MACCORKILL	MACNICOLL	TOLMIE
MACALLUM	MACCORKINDALE	MALCOLMSON	
MACASKIE	MACCORKLE	NICHOLL	

MACMILLAN (Map D7)   Believed to be of descent from Methlan, son of a 13th-century Buchanan chief, MacMillans became known about then around Loch Arkaig, with a branch by Loch Tay. From here in the 16th century their chief possession became Knapdale through marriage with a MacNeill heiress; and in Galloway also a branch developed who were later to achieve note as Covenanters.

At first dependent on the Lords of the Isles, the MacMillans afterwards lost their clan lands to bigger neighbours, the Lochaber group becoming fighting followers of the Camerons, whilst some from Knapdale avoided Campbell 'protection' by migrating to Arran. The Baxter sept claim descent from a Chief's son who once eluded pursuit by assuming the guise of a busy baker.

Septs:

BAXTER	BLUE	BROWN	MACNAMELL
BELL	BROUN	MACBAXTER	

MACNAB (Map F6)

MACNAB (Map F6)   The MacNabs are of ancient origin in Breadalbane and claim to be descended of Clan Alpin, also from a family of hereditary abbots of St Fillan's monastery once in Glendochart, hence *Mac an Aba*, 'Son of the abbot'. The old Celtic church did not stipulate celibacy. The Dewar sept long held custody of the beautiful Celtic 'Crozier of St Fillan', now in the Royal Museum of Scotland, Edinburgh. The Gaelic form of St Fillan is the origin of several sept names including Cleland and MacLellan for whom separate clanship has been claimed.

From their once extensive clan lands there remains only the MacNab burial island at Killin. The reduction arose through supporting MacDougalls against the unforgetting Bruce; and again for following Montrose, when their royalist Chief was taken prisoner and escaped only to fall at Worcester 1651 with many other Highlanders. A later kenspeckle Chief was the subject of Raeburn's jaunty portrait *The MacNab*.

Septs:

ABBOT	CLELLAND	GILLAND	MACCLELLAND
ABBOTSON	DEWAR	GILLILAND	MACNABB
ABBOTT	GILFILLAN	MACCLELLAND	MACNAIR
CLELAND	GILLAN	MACLELLAN	

MACNAUGHTON (Map E6)

MACNAUGHTON (Map E6)   With the ancient name Nechtan, borne by four Pictish kings, the MacNaughtons claim as progenitor a chief of one of the powerful Moray tribes transplanted by Malcolm IV. This Nachtan Mor and his clan he settled in Strathtay and Strathspey, but within a century we find them migrating again to greater power in Argyll, with charters to their chief seat at Dunderave on Loch Fyne and another stronghold, Fraoch Eilean, in Loch Awe. Other fortresses of Dun Nachtan in Lewis and Strathspey recall their wide-ranged influence. This became severely reduced from the clan's joining the various Stewart risings.

Septs:

HENDERSON	MACHENDRY	MACNAUCHTON	MACQUAKER
HENDRIE	MACHENRY	MACNAUGHT	MACVICAR
HENDRY	MACKENDRICK	MACNAUGHTAN	NEVIN
HENRY	MACKENRICK	MACNAYER	NEVISON
KENDRICK	MACKNIGHT	MACNEUR	NIVEN
KENRICK	MACMATH	MACNEVIN	NIVISON
MACBRAYNE	MACNACHTAN	MACNIVEN	PORTER
MACCRACKEN	MACNAGHTEN	MACNUIR	WEIR
MACHENDRIE	MACNAIR	MACNUYER	

MACNEIL (Map A4, A5, D7)

MACNEIL (Map A4, A5, D7)   Niall, Nigel or Neil, the clan's founder in Bruce's reign, had lands in Knapdale and Kintyre and was probably of Clan Donald stock. MacNeills in Galloway at least as early as Bruce may be of the ancient Irish O'Neills. The MacNeil clan at first followed the Lords of the Isles, then after 1493 the two separated braches of Barra and Gigha took opposite sides with the MacLeans and Islay MacDonalds respectively. Neil's great-grandson was in 1427 granted Barra, the Hebridean isle with its forbidding islet-castle

Kisimul, and South Uist. Torquil MacNeill, about the same time, founded the branch-clan of Gigha, also of Taynish and Colonsay.

The clan's maritime tradition appears in *The Highland Fair*, Mitchell's ballad-opera of 1731, when the Bardess omits Noah from one long genealogy: 'The MacNeil had a boat of its own!' And one of the clan was chief designer of the Cunarders *Queen Mary* and *Queen Elizabeth*.

Septs:

MACGOUGAN	MACNEALE	NEAL	NELSON
MACGRAIL	MACNEILAGE	NEALE	NIEL
MACGUGAN	MACNEILL	NEIL	NIELSON
MACGUIGAN	MACNELLY	NEILL	
MACNEAL	MACNIEL	NEILSON	

MACPHERSON (Map G4)   The name means 'Son of the Parson', one Murriach or Murdoch who in 1153 succeeded to the Chiefship of Clan Chattan (see thereunder) and obtained special dispensation to marry. His third son evinced a skill that established one source of the numerous Smith families. Previously of Lochaber, the MacPhersons were settled in Badenoch by Robert Bruce on land they had wrested from his Comyn rivals. A great quarrel with the Davidsons was settled by winning that 1396 combat of the North Inch of Perth, with the help of Hal Gow o' the Wynd — also doubtless by playing the clan's Fairy Chanter.

After Culloden, Cluny MacPherson shared his Benalder 'Cage' for weeks with Prince Charlie and remained himself in hiding for nine years. Despite large rewards offered, the loyal clansmen betrayed neither. James MacPherson (1738-96), with his version of Ossian's epic that first directed world attention to Celtic legends, instigated a new era of 'Romantic' taste.

Septs:

ARCHIBALD	GILLESPIE	MACCLEISH	MACLERIE
CATTANACH	GILLIE	MACCURRACH	MACLISE
CLARK	GILLIES	MACCURRIE	MACLISH
CLARKE	GOUDIE	MACGILLIES	MACMURDO
CLARKSON	GOW	MACGOUN	MACMURDOCH
CLERK	GOWAN	MACGOW	MACMURRICH
CLUNIE	GOWANS	MACGOWAN	MACVURICH
CLUNY	LEARY	MACKEITH	MACVURRICH
CURRIE	LEES	MACLEAR	MURDOCH
ELLIS	MACCHLERY	MACLEARY	MURDOSON
ELLISON	MACCLAIR	MACLEES	PEARSON
FERSEN	MACCLEARY	MACLEISH	SMITH

MACQUARRIE (Map C5)   The name is from Guarie or Godfrey, and the MacQuarries claim Clan Alpin descent from his being a brother to the Fingon, reputed founder of the Clan MacKinnon. Settled since at least the 13th century in the Isle of Ulva and the neighbouring part of Mull, until 1493 the clan followed the Lords of the Isles, thereafter the MacLeans of Duart. The last Chief joined the army aged 63, dying aged 103 in 1818. The name is prominent on Australian maps, from a clansman who was long Governor of New South Wales. An earlier one founded the Irish MacGuires.

Septs:

MACCORRIE	MACGORRIE	MACQUAIRE	MACQUIRE
MACCORRY	MACGUARIE	MACQUARIE	QUARRY
MACGORRY	MACGUIRE	MACQUHIRR	WHARRIE

MACQUEEN (Map C3)   Originally of Skye as a small sept of the great MacDonalds, the Clan Macqueen or MacSweyn derives from some ancestor of the Norse name Sweyn. The Castle and Loch Sween in Knapdale were named from a 13th-century branch which later became absorbed by MacMillans and Lamonts. The chief branch, or Clan Revan, migrated via Moidart to Strathdearn by the River Findhorn. Here, with their chief Revan MacMulmor MacSweyn, they settled about 1410 as a contingent of Clan Chattan under Macintosh leadership. Some Irish forms of the name are of non-Norse origin, and if meaning 'son of Conn' may again relate them to the legendary Celtic ancestor of Clan Donald.

Septs:	MACSWAIN	MACSWEEN	REVANS
	MACSWAN	MACWHAN	SWAN

MACRAE (Map E4)   The Clan Macrae are first heard of settled at Clunes, near Beauly. In the 14th century, through quarrels with the Frasers of that locality, they accompanied their neighbours the MacLennans across Ross-shire to Kintail. Settled in the mountain-encircled Glenshiel, the Macraes commanded Loch Alsh from the fortress of Eilean Donan, restored by a 20th-century Chief, still its hereditary Constable. The name belongs to a small class of 'Macs' not meaning the son of some ancestor. The earliest form, Macrath, was a baptismal term, translated as 'Son of grace', or 'of good-fortune'. Other names for the clan have been 'the Wild Macraes' and, from long adherence with the MacKenzies, 'Seaforth's Mail-shirt'.

Septs:

CRAE	MACCRAW	MACGRATH	MACRAY
CREE	MACCRAY	MACGRAW	MACRIE
MACARA	MACCREA	MACHRAY	RAE
MACARRA	MACCREATH	MACRA	RAITH
MACCRA	MACCREE	MACRACH	RAY
MACCRACH	MACCRIE	MACRAITH	REA
MACCRAE	MACCROW	MACRATH	REATH
MACCRAITH	MACCROY	MACRAW	

MACTHOMAS (Map I5)   Founded by Thomas, a natural son of Angus, sixth Chief of Clan Macintosh in the 14th century. A clan MacThomas appears in a list of Clans belonging to the Ancient Federation of Clan Chattan. In a later role (1587) there occurs 'Clan MacThomas in Glenshee'.

Septs:

McCOMAS	MACCOMIE	TAMSON	THOMASON
McCOMB	McHAMISH	THOM	THOMS
MACCOMBIE	MACTHOMAS	THOMAS	THOMSON

MALCOLM (Map D4, D7)   The name means a Devotee of St Columba, the founder of Iona and missionary to the Northern Picts. Borne by four Scottish kings, it early became a favourite Christian name and then surname in various parts of Scotland. One family of Malcolms had charters of Stirlingshire lands from the 14th century.

The Highland clan is by tradition a branch of the MacGillechallums, otherwise MacLeods of Raasay. From the early 15th century they became established in the Loch Awe district under Campbell leadership.

Septs:	CALLAM	MACALLUM	MALCOLM
	CALLUM	MACCALLUM	

MATHESON (Map E4)   The Celtic clan MacMaghan or MacMathan, otherwise Clan of the Bear, once held a powerful position in Wester Ross. Tradition claims they assisted Kenneth MacAlpin in 843 against the Picts, also that the old Earls of Ross and the Clan MacKenzie came from their stock. They were Constables of Eilean Donan Castle before the Macraes. From feuds with neighbours they became much reduced and dispersed, and from the 15th century followed the MacKenzie banner. Confusion arises from their adopting, about that time, the somewhat similar south-country name Matheson, really Matthew-son, itself an old name in Scotland under various forms.

Septs:

BAIRNSON	MACMAHON	MASSIE	MATHIESON
MACBIRNIE	MACMATH	MATTHEWSON	
MACBURNIE	MASSEY	MATHIE	

MAXWELL (Map H8)   The name is from lands called after Maccus'-well, a fishing-reach of the River Tweed by Kelso. The Border clan might have derived from Maccus, a 10th-century king of Man and the Isles, but more likely from some Norman family settled there by Malcolm Canmore and destined to hold many high offices thereafter. From being Sheriffs of Teviotdale, their chief territory became Nithsdale from the 13th century and the Solway castle of Caerlaverock their headquarters. Frequently Wardens of the West March, they were fully engaged in the border struggles, and the fourth Lord Maxwell fell at Flodden. Among their more private feuds, the Johnstons were their chief adversaries. James Clerk Maxwell in 1865 first explained the feasability of radio transmission.

MENZIES (Map H5, G5)   The 'z' comes from erroneous copying of the old written 'y', and even without that, the pronunciation has varied considerably, from *Meinn* in the Gaelic to 'Men-yes', 'Ming-us', etc. The Perthshire clan took its name from the de Meyners (in England becoming Manners), one of the many Norman families installed around the 12th century to organise the people, whether for peace or war. Without being missing from Bannockburn or Prince Charlie's ranks and events between, the Menzies earned their chief repute constructively. 'The fat herds of the Menzies' were well quoted by other clans, whilst the Araucarian Pine ('Monkey puzzle') and more usefully widespread larch were each introduced to Scotland by a Menzies about two centuries ago. The clan itself spread widely. From Atholl and Breadalbane offshoots reached Nithsdale, Lanarkshire, Kippen, Aberdeenshire and Fife.

Septs:

DEWAR	MACMINN	MEIN	MINNUS
MACINDEOR	MACMONIES	MEINE	
MACMENZIES	MEANIES	MENGUES	
MACMIN	MEANS	MINN	

MORRISON (Map C2)   The Morrisons shared Lewis in the Hebrides with their earliest neighbours the MacLeods and the MacAulays. They took their name from a chief Maurice, after being earlier known as MacGilmore from some 'son of a devotee of Mary', but the change occurred before the Reformation. For a period ending with the MacKenzies taking charge of Lewis in 1613, Morrisons held the strenuous post of hereditary Brieve, or arbitrating judge, in the 'Long Isle', though in face of the powerful MacLeods this was a source rather of feud than of justice. Branches of the clan became settled in Harris, Skye, the Northwest mainland, and Aberdeenshire. A Perthshire group claim as its ancestor the Buchanan Clan's Maurice.

Septs:

	BRIEVE	GILMOUR	MACBRIEVE
	GILMORE	JUDGE	MORISON

MUNRO (Map G3)   Tradition gives the Munros an Irish origin, from the river Roe in Derry, but for about eight centuries now their Chiefs have been Munro of Foulis, on the Cromarty Firth, established there as vassals of the Earls of Ross until that overlordship was removed in 1476. They were with Bruce at Bannockburn. Although friendly to Mary Queen of Scots, Munros became ardent Protestants, like the MacKays, and acquired army distinction with Gustavus Adolphus in Sweden and at home on behalf of governments clearly of their own religious persuasion.

James Monroe, fifth U.S. President, was descended from one of these 17th-century soldiers, whilst Edinburgh's prestige in medicine was first established by 'the Monro Dynasty', three successive professors named Alexander Monro, the first born in 1697, the third dying in 1859.

Septs:

DINGWALL	KIDDIE	MACKEDDIE	MUNROE
FOULIS	MACADIE	MACLULLICH	VASS
FOWLIS	MACCULLOCH	MONRO	WASS
KEDDIE	MACEDDIE	MONROE	

MURRAY (Map H6, G2)   Though a few among the Galloway Murrays may derive from 'MacMurray', most by far of this widespread clan take their name from the ancient province of Moray, which once included Inverness-shire besides the present county, and in the 12th century was the storm-centre of a series of clan rebellions against the nationally organised feudalism of Malcolm Canmore's dynasty. Under David I the 1130 revolt was suppressed and a process begun of transplanting whole clans into and out of Moray. Freskin of Strathbrock (Broxburn), said to be a Fleming, was one of the incoming leaders. He was installed at Duffus with the name de Moravia and is claimed as founder to all Clan Murray. The earliest branches were of Sutherland and Bothwell, and an important Perthshire section includes the Duke of Atholl as Chief of the Tullibardine branch. Murrays took a prominent place with Wallace and Bruce and in both Jacobite risings, as also in other spheres, such as founding the scientific Royal Society of London. The various Earls of Moray had little or no connection with the Clan Murray.

Septs:

BALNEAVES	FLEMING	PIPER	SMALL
DINSMORE	MORAY	PYPER	SMEAL
DUNBAR	MURRIE	SMAIL	SPALDING
DUNSMORE	NEAVES	SMALE	

OGILVIE (Map J5, J3)   The Ogilvies descend from Gilchrist, first Earl of Angus, through his second son Gilbert, who about 1170 was granted the barony of Ogilvie near Glamis and took his name from it. Chiefship lies with the Airlie branch — 'the Bonnie Hoose' of Jacobite song. Their devotion to the Stewarts led to feuds with various neighbours like the Campbells of Dollar, and the Banffshire Ogilvies against the Gordons. The Lord Ogilvie who was exiled for his share of 'the forty-five' received command of a regiment of pre-revolutionary France that took his name.

Septs:

AIRLIE	GILCHRIST	OGILVY	STORRIE
FINDLATER	MACGILCHRIST	RICHARDSON	
FUTHIE	OGILBY	STOREY	

ROBERTSON (Map G5) Their first chief Duncan, from whom the numerous Robertsons take their alternative name Clan Donnachaidh or Donnachie, was friend and ally to King Robert Bruce and tradition had him a son of the Angus Mor mentioned under the MacDonalds. The clan remained ever active and loyal to the Stewarts and took the new name from their chief Robert (himself named after Bruce), to commemorate his capturing the murderers of James I in 1437. From the name of their ancient seat in Atholl the Chiefs retain the style Struan Robertson, but branches became distributed widely in Scotland and, indeed, throughout the world.

Septs:

COLLIER	DONAGHY	MACDONACHIE	MACROBIE
COLYEAR	DUNCAN	MACGLASHAN	MACWILLIAM
CONNOCHIE	DUNCANSON	MACINROY	REED
CONOCHIE	DUNNACHIE	MACIVER	REID
CUNNISON	HOBSON	MACIVOR	ROBBIE
DOBBIE	INCHES	MACJAMES	ROBERTS
DOBBIN	KYNOCH	MACLAGAN	ROBISON
DOBIE	MACCONACHIE	MACCULLICH	ROBSON
DOBIESON	MACCONCHIE	MACONACHIE	ROY
DOBINSON	MACCONICH	MACROBBIE	STARK
DOBSON	MACCONECHY	MACROBERT	TONNOCHY
DONACHIE	MACCONNOCHIE	MACROBERTS	

ROSE (Map H3) Around the 12th century the Norman family de Ros acquired lands in various parts of Scotland; and a small Strathnairn clan, first recorded in Alexander II's time at Geddes, early became Rose of Kilravock (pronounced 'Ross of Kilraik'). By cleverly simple diplomacy and studiously planting their own garden — as observed for instance by visitors Prince Charlie, and Cumberland the day after — the chiefs achieved respect, safety and an unbroken succession through long centuries amid contending factions. The family talent must have clung to the J. A. Rose who attained rank in the French Revolution government while saving many lives from its 'Terror', playing a role greater than his fictional counterpart 'the Scarlet Pimpernel'.

Septs:

BARON	BARRON	GEDDES	ROSS

ROSS (Map G3) The Norman family de Ros were established in North Ayrshire in the 12th century and from the same quarter installed a fresh branch over two centuries ago by purchasing the Balnagowan seat of the unrelated Clan Ross chiefs. Hence many Rosses in the south, in the Moray to Aberdeen sector, and some in Ross-shire itself are really of the same ancestry as Clan Rose, pronounced also Ross.

The Ross clan, otherwise Anrias from a 13th-century chief MacGilleAndreas, 'Son of a devotee of St Andrew', took name from the province of which their earliest chiefs were Earls. They served with Bruce at Bannockburn and came to possess a large section of Ross-shire but lost much power after Harlaw 1411 (Map J5) and the 1476 forfeiture of the earldom to the crown. In more recent times Rosses have earned front rank in such spheres as polar exploration and tropical medicine.

Septs:

ANDERSON	DENOON	HAGGART	TAGGART
ANDISON	DENUNE	MACANDREW	TULLO
ANDREW	DINGWALL	MACCULLIE	TULLOCH
ANDREWS	DUTHIE	MACCULLOCH	TYRE
CORBET	FAIR	MACLULLICH	VASS
CORBETT	GAIR	MACTAGGART	WASS
CROW	GEAR	MACTEAR	
CROWE	GILLANDERS	MACTIER	
CROY	HAGART	MACTIRE	

SCOTT (Map I8)   The first recorded of this surname, originally spelt Scot, was Uchtred filius Scoti ('Son of a Scot', i.e. not Saxon or Norman) about 1124, and his grandsons are believed to have founded the branches of Buccleuch and Balwearie in Fife, from which in turn came many others and a noted clan of the Border. The great Sir Walter is far from the only brilliant star among 'the Saucy Scotts'. Michael Scot, 'the Wizard' of Balwearie, contemporary scientist with the 13th-century Roger Bacon, then the 17th-century Sir John Scot of Scotstarvit, another sane eccentric, and David Scott, among our finest painters, are three that merit fuller appreciation.

Septs:

GEDDES   LAIDLAW   LANGLANDS   NAPIER

SHAW (Map H4)   The Highland Shaws were a branch of Clan Chattan and claim descent from the 12th-century Seach or Shiach mentioned as founder of the Macintosh clan. First settled at Rothiemurchus in Strathspey, with an islet-fortress in Loch nan Eilean, the clan became broken up when their Chief of 1595 was dispossessed. Sections attached themselves to Macintosh and MacPherson, whilst many migrated over the Lairig Ghru into Aberdeenshire. The playwright George Bernard Shaw descended of a Dublin branch. The name Shaw was then adopted as sounding like the original Gaelic, but in the Lowlands it means 'a small wood' and has been a family surname in Renfrewshire since the 13th century, with its own branches spreading later to Stirlingshire and through Ayrshire to Galloway.

Septs:

	MACKAY	SEATH	SHEACH
	MACHAY	SETH	SHIACH

SINCLAIR (Map I2)   The St Clairs first arrived in England with William the Conqueror, then in the Scotland of David I a branch became settled at Roslin, near Edinburgh. From 1379 these gave name to Scotland's most northerly clan and acquired its chiefship by a marriage to the heiress of the earldom of Caithness. Apart from local feuds with the Gunns and others, Sinclairs have frequently distinguished themselves in Scottish history. One Sir William fell in Spain, 1330, with the Douglas who was bearing Bruce's heart to the Holy Land. Then to Sinclairs green is counted unlucky since so many of them wearing it fell with their Chief at Flodden, 1513. Sir John Sinclair of Ulbster, painted by Raeburn as Commander of the Fencible Regiment he raised in 1794, was a most practical idealist, forerunner of social surveys and planned agriculture and first to use the word 'statistics'.

Septs:

	BUDGE	GROAT	WARES
	CLYNE	LYALL	

SKENE (Map K4)   The Skenes took their name from the place in Aberdeenshire they had occupied for some time before Robert Bruce in 1317 granted Robert de Skene a baronial charter. W. F. Skene, the 19th-century historian of the Celts, believed his ancestor, this Robert, to be descended from an early Chief of Clan Robertson. Skene chiefs fell in several national battles, at Harlaw, Flodden and Pinkie.

Septs:

DYAS   DYCE   SKEEN

STEWART (Map F7, H6, H8)   The surname Stewart is the same as Steward, indicating the offical in charge of the household and treasury, whether of the king or of some court-holding earl or bishop. It was from Walter fitz Alan, the Norman noble appointed by David I hereditary High Steward of Scotland with personal estates in Renfrewshire, that the Stewart kings descended. But Walter's influential family and descendants had established various separate branches of Stewarts before their main line attained its Royal status. This occurred through another Walter, the sixth High Steward, who fought at Bannockburn, marrying King Robert Bruce's daughter Marjory. Their son became Robert II, the first Stewart king, when David II died childless in 1371. From then on the Stewart dynasty's strengths and weaknesses, self-sacrificing leadership mingled with unremitting obstinacies, brought no little of the clan spirit into national history.

Previous to 1371, Walter's uncle, Sir John Stewart of Bonkill, who fell at Falkirk 1298, left seven sons. The first three founded respectively the Stewart earldoms of Angus, Lennox, and Galloway.

Septs:

BOYD	FRANCIS	LYLE	MOODIE
CARMICHAEL	LENNOX	MACMICHAEL	MOODY
DENNISON	LISLE	MENTEITH	STEUARD
DENNISTON	LOMBARD	MONTEATH	STEUART
FRANCE	LUMBARD	MONTEITH	STUART

STEWART of Appin (Map E5)   Sir John's fourth son, Sir James Stewart of Pierston and Warwickhill, Ayrshire, who fell at Halidon Hill 1333, became ancestor to several important lines, including the Stewart Lords of Lorne and those of Atholl. The Appin clan sprang from the last Lord Lorne, who died in 1469.

Septs:

CARMICHAEL	LIVINGSTON	MACDONLEAVY	MACNAIRN
CLAY	LIVINGSTONE	MACKINDLAY	MACNUCATOR
COMBE	LORNE	MACKINLAY	MACROB
COMBICH	MACCLAY	MACKINLEY	MACROBB
COMBIE	MACCLEAY	MACLAE	MITCHELL
CONLAY	MACCOLL	MACLAY	MITCHELSON
CONLEY	MACCOMBE	MACLEA	ROBB
DONLEVY	MACCOMBICH	MACLEAY	WALKER
LEAY	MACCOMBIE	MACLEW	
LEVACK	MACCOMIE	MACMICHAEL	

STEWART of Atholl (Map G5, H5)   The first Stewart Earl of Atholl was Sir John of Balveny, son of Sir James Stewart, 'the Black Knight of Lorne', and Jane, widow of King James I of Scotland. But around the same time, most of the Atholl clan sprang from five sons of Sir Alexander Stewart, fourth son of Robert II, and most markedly remembered as the fierce 'Wolf of Badenoch', who died 1404.

Septs:

CONACHER	CRUIKSHANK	GRAY	MACGARROW
CRUICKSHANK	DUILACH	LARNACH	MACGLASHAN
CRUICKSHANKS	GARROW	LARNACK	

STUART of Bute (Map E7)   The beautiful Isle of Bute formed part of the domain of Walter, the first High Steward, and remained a Stewart possession except for a brief Norse occupation. But only after 1385 did a family branch become established there, when Sir John Stewart, a son of King Robert II, was appointed hereditary Sheriff of Bute and Arran. His descendants still hold the marquisate of Bute.

The spelling 'Stuart' originated with some Stewarts living in France where the alphabet has no 'w'. Adopted there also by Mary Queen of Scots, it became fashionable when she continued using it on her return. Steuart was a compromise between the two forms.

Septs:

BALLANTYNE	JAMIESON	MACELHERAN	MALLOY
BANNATYNE	LEWIS	MACKERRON	MILLOY
CAW	LOY	MACKIRDY	MUNN
FULLARTON	MACCAA	MACLEWIS	NEILSON
FULLERTON	MACCAMMIE	MACLOUIS	SHARP
GLASS	MACCAW	MACLOY	SHARPE
HUNTER	MACCLOY	MACMUNE	
JAMESON	MACCURDY	MACMURTRIE	

SUTHERLAND (Map G2)   The Clan Sutherland is an early branch from Clan Murray, as there mentioned. In 1197 Hugh, a grandson of Freskin de Moravia, was granted by William the Lion the southern portion of Caithness, named *Sudrland* while previously under Norse occupation. Hugh's son William, who died at Dunrobin Castle in 1248, was created Earl of Sutherland, which earldom remains the oldest extant in Britain.

The clan, of whom many retained the name Murray, was much embroiled in feuds with neighbours until a peace of 1591, yet figured with distinction at Bannockburn and other national battles. In the Jacobite times they took the side of government along with old rivals like the MacKays, and in contrast to their own parent clan. In 1800 they formed the 93rd or Sutherland Highlanders — the 'Thin Red Line' of Balaclava — that was joined with the Argyllshires in 1881.

Septs:

CHIENE	DUFFES	GRAY	MOWATT
CHEYNE	DUFFUS	KEITH	MURRAY
CLYNE	FEDERITH	MOUAT	OLIPHANT

URQUHART (Map G3)   By tradition a very early branch from Clan Forbes, the small clan Urquhart took their name from the glen and fortress by Loch Ness that they occupied, although also settled in Cromarty as hereditary Sheriffs from at least the 14th century. Sir Thomas Urquhart of Cromarty, the celebrated translator of Rabelais, was a devoted warrior for both Charles I and Charles II and died from a fit of laughter on hearing of the latter's Restoration in 1660.

THE SCOTTISH TARTANS

There are two main schools of thought on the origin of tartans. One view is that way back in the mists of time every Scottish family had a distinctive tartan pattern, the colours of which were obtained from the plants which grew only in their locality. The opposing view states that clans, kilts and tartan were an early 19th-century invention which the Victorians developed into an enormous cult. Somewhere between these two schools lies the truth.

What is well recorded is that the Celts were noted for their exuberant sense of colour, Roman observers referring to their striped, variegated or chequered clothing and tattoos. The simple two-colour checks of two thousand years ago have evolved through a progression of cross-checks into a profusion of differing patterns which today themselves number well over two thousand. 'Tartan' itself is a word originally imported from Europe, the Gaels using the term *breacan*, meaning 'speckled' or 'multicoloured'. The word 'plaid' is from the Gaelic word for blanket, being either a bedcover or a length of cloth perhaps 12 feet by 5 feet which was swathed around the wearer and belted at the waist, hence the term 'belted plaid'. The essentially white-based, patterned household blankets which went with the early Scots settlers to North America evoked an admiration for the pretty 'plaid patterns', and in time 'plaid' itself became a synonym for tartan and of arguably older origin.

Gaelic poetry and recorded observations, back to at least the 16th century, associate certain setts of tartan with specific families, but no more than a handful. However, tartan was of sufficient importance by the time of the 1745 Rising that its aftermath saw a severely shaken government rush through an Act of Parliament in 1746 which banned the wearing of 'tartan, kilt and plaid' by all civilian men and boys other than landowners. That Act was not repealed until 1782, and in the ensuing period of restoration for Scotland's shattered pride a series of cultural traditions were revived or invented which served to confuse the historical realities concerning what was to become the national dress for all Scotland.

Tartans and Highland dress were not regimented until the Scottish regiments themselves adopted standard-pattern uniforms, and quaint Victorian customs such as the wearing of 'dress' tartans after 6 p.m. do not detract from the venerable pedigree of non-military Highland dress, stretching back at least three hundred years.

It is an old Highland tradition to encourage guests to wear our unique mode of dress. We should regard it as a compliment. For the wearer who has no tartan associated with his surname, there are certain options available:

1. Wear that which is connected to your maternal or any other of your family lines.
2. Wear the sett appropriate to the district from which your family comes or in which your surname was known.
3. Wear the Jacobite or Caledonian setts, or even the Government or 'Black Watch' pattern if you are not pro-Stuart.
4. Wear whichever you prefer, but remember that when you sport a tartan you are proclaiming allegiance to that chief and his clan. Your loyalties may be tested!

ABERDEEN
ANDERSON
ANGUS
ARMSTRONG
ATHOLL DISTRICT
AUSTIN (and KEITH)
BAIRD
BALMORAL
BARCLAY
Dress BARCLAY
BLACK WATCH (42nd Regimental)
BLAIR LOGIE
BRODIE
Hunting BRODIE
BRUCE

BUCHANAN
CAMERON
CAMERON of Erracht
CAMERON of Lochiel
CAMPBELL of Argyll
Dress CAMPBELL of Argyll
CAMPBELL of Breadalbane
CAMPBELL of Cawdor
CAMPBELL of Loudoun
CARNEGIE
CHISHOLM
Hunting CHISHOLM
CLERGY
COCKBURN
COLQUHOUN

CRANSTON
CRAWFORD
CRIEFF
CUMMING
Hunting CUMMING
CUNNINGHAM
DALZIEL
DAVIDSON
DAVIDSON of Tulloch
DOUGLAS
DOUGLAS (Grey)
DRUMMOND (Same as GRANT)
Old DRUMMOND
DRUMMOND of Strathallan
DUNBAR
DUNBLANE
DUNCAN
DUNDAS
DUNDEE
DYCE
EDINBURGH
ELLIOT
ERSKINE
FARQUHARSON
FERGUSON
FERGUSON of Balquhidder
FLETCHER
FLETCHER of Dunans
FORBES
FORT WILLIAM
FORTY-SECOND (BLACK WATCH)
Dress FORTY-SECOND
FRASER
Hunting FRASER
GALLOWAY DISTRICT
Dress GALLOWAY (Red)
Hunting GALLOWAY (Green)
GLASGOW
GLEN LYON DISTRICT
GLEN ORCHY DISTRICT
GORDON
Dress GORDON
Old GORDON
GOW and MACGOWAN
GRAHAM of Monteith
GRAHAM of Montrose
GRANT
GRANT of Glenmoriston
GUNN
Old GUNN
HAMILTON
HAY
HENDERSON and MACKENDRICK
HOME
HOPE-VERE
HUNTLY DISTRICT

INNES
JACOBITE
JOHNSTON
KEITH and AUSTIN
KENNEDY
KERR
LAMONT
LAUDER
LEITH-HAY
LENNOX
LESLIE
Dress LESLIE (Red)
LINDSAY
LIVINGSTONE
LOGAN or MACLENNAN
MACALISTER
MACALPINE
MACARTHUR
MACAULAY
Hunting MACAULAY
MACBEAN
MACBETH
MACCALLUM
Old MACCALLUM
MACDIARMID
MACDONALD of the Isles
Dress MACDONALD of the Isles
Old MACDONALD of the Isles
MACDONALD of Sleat
Dress MACDONALD of Sleat
Old MACDONALD of Sleat
MACDONALD (or MACIAN) of
    Ardnamurchan
MACDONALD of Clanranald
Hunting MACDONALD of Clanranald
MACDONALD of Kingsburgh
MACDONALD of Staffa (or Boisdale)
MACDONNELL of Glengarry
Hunting MACDONNELL of Glengarry
MACDONNELL of Keppoch
MACDOUGALL
MACDUFF
Hunting MACDUFF
MACEWAN
MACFARLANE
MACFARLANE (Black and White)
MACFIE
MACGILLIVRAY
MACGOWAN or GOW
MACGREGOR
MACGREGOR Rob Roy
MACHARDY
MACIAN (See MACDONALD)
MACINNES
Hunting MACINNES
MACINROY

MACINTOSH
MACINTYRE
Dress MACINTYRE (Red)
MACINTYRE of Glenorchy
MACIVOR
MACKAY
MACKENDRICK or HENDERSON
MACKENZIE
MACKINLAY
MACKINNON
Hunting MACKINNON
MACLACHLAN
Dress MACLACHLAN
Old MACLACHLAN
MACLAINE of Lochbuie
Hunting MACLAINE of Lochbuie
MACLAREN
MACLEAN of Duart
Hunting MACLEAN of Duart
MACLENNAN or LOGAN
MACLEOD of Harris (and of Skye)
MACLEOD of Harris (Black and white)
MACLEOD of Harris (Black and red)
MACLEOD of Lewis (and of Raasay and
    Assynt)
Dress MACLEOD of Lewis
MACMILLAN
Hunting MACMILLAN
MACNAB
MACNAUGHTON
MACNEIL of Barra
MACNEILL of Gigha (and of Colonsay)
MACNICOL or NICOLSON
MACPHERSON
Old 'Hunting' MACPHERSON (Grey
    ground)
Dress MACPHERSON (White)
MACQUARRIE
MACQUEEN
MACRAE (Green)
Dress MACRAE (Red)
Hunting MACRAE
MACRAE of Conchra
MACTAGGART
MACTAVISH
MACTHOMAS (Ancient and Modern)
MALCOLM
MATHESON
Hunting MATHESON
MAXWELL
MELVILLE
MENZIES (Red and white)
MENZIES (Black and red)
MENZIES (Black and white)
Hunting MENZIES
MIDDLETON

MONTGOMERY
Old MONTGOMERY
MORRISON
MOUAT
MULL DISTRICT
MUNRO
Dress MUNRO (Red)
MURRAY of Atholl
MURRAY of Tullibardine
NAPIER
NICOLSON or MACNICOL
OGILVIE
Hunting OGILVIE (Green)
OLIPHANT
PAISLEY
RAMSAY
RATTRAY
ROB ROY (MacGregor)
ROBERTSON
Hunting ROBERTSON
ROSE
Dress ROSE (Red)
ROSS
Hunting ROSS
ROXBURGH DISTRICT
RUSSELL
RUTHVEN
SCOTT
Hunting SCOTT
SCOTT (Black and white)
SINCLAIR
Hunting SINCLAIR
SKENE
SKENE (Yellow stripe)
Royal STEWART (Red)
Royal STEWART (White, Prince
    Charles Edward)
Dress STEWART
Hunting STEWART
STEWART (Black ground)
STEWART (Black and white)
STEWART of Appin
Old STEWART of Appin
STEWART of Atholl
STEWART of Galloway
STUART of Bute
STRATHEARN
SUTHERLAND
Old SUTHERLAND
TWEEDSIDE DISTRICT
URQUHART
Old URQUHART
WALLACE
Old WALLACE
WEMYSS
Old WEMYSS

THE CLAN MAP OF SCOTLAND

A brief description, with key to each illustration in the map

Key

A1 THE LION RAMPANT The Scottish Lion, as worn on Royal and princely shields.

A3 THE HARP OF THE HEBRIDES In early times the harp was the principal musical instrument.

A4 HIGHLAND CATTLE These strong, shaggy animals are natives of the Highlands and are to be seen grazing on the hillsides and plains, looking as picturesque as their rugged surroundings.

A7 JOHN KNOX AT HOLYROOD PALACE When Mary Queen of Scots returned from France in 1561, after thirteen years' absence, she tried to re-establish the Roman Catholic Religion. John Knox, a native of Haddington, and an outstanding figure during the Reformation, preached in St Giles Cathedral against her practices. She summoned him to Holyrood and used every argument against him, but she soon found that he was to be her most bitter enemy during her reign and that the Reformed Church was firmly established.

A8 HOLYROOD ABBEY The Abbey was built by King David I in 1128. The ruined Church still remains. Here took place the marriages of James II, James III, and James IV, and that of Queen Mary and Lord Darnley. It contains the graves of kings and queens of Scotland, and many other distinguished persons. In 1429, James I received, from the High Altar, the submission of Alexander, Lord of the Isles.

A9 MARY QUEEN OF SCOTS AT HOLYROOD PALACE A halo of romance surrounds Mary Queen of Scots and Holyrood. Her life there was one of splendour and gaiety. She was one of the most beautiful women of her time. By her fearless courage and winsome manners, she made many friends, but her impulsiveness and indiscretion often brought trouble upon her and endangered the lives of others. Her lover, Rizzio, was murdered in the Palace, and from here she fled with Bothwell after the unfortunate death of her husband, Darnley.

B2 THE LORD OF THE ISLES AND HIS CHIEFS The MacDonalds, Lords of the Isles and Earls of Ross, descended from Somerled, son of Gilliebride, of the 11th century. They represented a race of famous warriors, their influence and power being so great at one period as to threaten the Scottish king. The clans of the Western Isles and the greater part of the Highlands were under their domination until the 13th century.

B5 THE PIPERS The MacCruimins were the most celebrated pipers in the Highlands. They were Hereditary Pipers to the MacLeods. 'Oil-Thigh', a college, was kept by them for the instruction of pipe music. They have many compositions to their illustrious name.

B6 SAINT COLUMBA Saint Columba arrived on our shores, on the island of Iona, in 563. He set up the first Celtic Church there and prepared his twelve apostles for the spreading of the Christian religion. He was connected with the Royal House of Leinster and the Kings of Dalriada.

B8 HOLYROOD PALACE The Palace was founded by James IV, in 1501, and was the residence of the Scottish Kings. It has witnessed many splendid gatherings. The Picture Gallery, the largest apartment of the Palace, was the scene of much splendour when 'Bonnie Prince Charlie' held his levées and balls there in 1745.

C4   **PRINCE CHARLES BIDS FAREWELL TO FLORA MACDONALD** Through the calmness, courage and devotion of a young lady, Flora MacDonald, Prince Charles made good his miraculous escape, from Benbecula to Skye, from the very presence of his pursuers. Dressed as her Irish serving maid, he was conducted by her to friends who conveyed him to a more secure hiding-place on the mainland until his escape to France could be made possible.

C8   **MARY QUEEN OF SCOTS IN LOCH LEVEN CASTLE** After the death of Darnley, her husband, Queen Mary was imprisoned in Loch Leven Castle. She was made to sign a document whereby she abdicated the Scottish throne in favour of her son, James. On the death of Elizabeth, Queen of England, James ascended the English throne, thus uniting the two crowns.

C9   **MARY QUEEN OF SCOTS ESCAPES FROM LOCH LEVEN CASTLE** A page named William Douglas got possession of the keys of the Castle. He hurried to the Queen and bade her proceed to the outer gate while he locked the doors, thus preventing immediate pursuit. As they rowed to the mainland, Douglas threw the keys into the loch.

D1   **JAMES V VISITS THE CLANS** In 1540 James V sailed to the Western Isles with twelve well-appointed ships carrying troops and artillery. The cabins were hung with silk and carried pavilions for erection wherever the King might choose to land. He made friends with many of the clan chiefs and invited them to join the Royal party, but afterwards betrayed them.

E3   **PRINCE CHARLES AND HIS FRIENDS** After the Battle of Culloden, Prince Charles made his way to the west coast. He went from place to place, and clan to clan, guarded and concealed by loyal Highlanders, while 500 regulars and militia combed the countryside for his capture. There was a reward of £30,000 on his head.

E4   **JAMES V MEETS THE CHIEFS** With pomp and splendour King James V visited the chiefs. He persuaded many of them to join the Royal tour, professing to be on the most friendly terms. When the ships reached Dumbarton, the King landed, but the chiefs, unsuspecting of the treachery of the King, were taken to Edinburgh, where they were imprisoned. Some remained there until the King's death,

E5   **RAISING THE STANDARD AT GLENFINNAN** On 23rd July 1745, Prince Charles Edward, grandson of the exiled King James, arrived on our shores to stir up the Jacobite cause. At the head of Loch Shiel, in the Valley of Glenfinnan, on 19th August, the Standard was raised by the aged Tullibardine, Duke of Atholl.

E6   **HIGHLAND DANCING** Highland Gatherings are held at different periods of the year at Oban, Dunoon, Luss, Braemar, Inverness, Aberdeen, etc. The day's programme includes Highland dancing, pipe music, sports and games. The March-past of the Pipers and the Highland Fling are favourite items.

F3   **THE FIERY CROSS** A cross made of wood, charred at one end, with a piece of white linen, dipped in goat's blood, hanging from the other represented the Fiery Cross, which was used as a symbol of war to call out the clans. Failure by a chief to obey its summons was punishable by death.

F5   **THE MASSACRE OF GLENCOE** In 1692 the MacDonalds of Glencoe were brutally attacked and massacred by the Campbells, who were given a signed order to extirpate the clan. One hundred and twenty of the MacDonalds, including the chief's two sons, escaped through the deep snow to the hills and glens.

F7   **THE BATTLE OF LARGS** The Norwegian army was defeated by Alexander III at the Battle of Largs in 1263, as a result of which Norway surrendered the Hebrides to Scotland on the payment of 4,000 marks and an agreed annual payment of 100 marks.

G2 **A NORSEMAN RAID**   These Vikings were a menace to Scotland in early times. They invaded her shores, plundered and burned the homes of the people, and carried off men, women and children as slaves.

G2 **CLAN BATTLE OF THE SUTHERLANDS**   Many clan battles were fought between legitimate heirs to titles and illegitimate sons. Such was the case in the 16th century in the history of the Sutherlands. The unfortunate son's head, after the battle, was hoisted on a spear on the tower of Dunrobin Castle. He had boasted that the witches had foretold 'that his head should be the highest that ever was of the Sutherlands'.

G3 **INVERNESS CASTLE**   The present Castle stands on the site of the ancient residence of the early Pictish Kings, this being the capital of the kingdom.

G4 **COLUMBA MEETS BRUDE**   Two years after Saint Columba arrived at Iona, he visited Brude, King of the Northern Picts, who readily became a convert to the new religion. The tribes followed the example of their King, and soon Columba's doctrine spread throughout Scotland.

G5 **WALLACE'S MONUMENT**   This monument was erected in 1869 to mark the defeat of the English in 1297 at the Battle of Stirling Bridge by William Wallace, a great Scottish hero. He was a native of Elderslie, near Paisley. The tower, which is 200 feet high, commands a magnificent view of the 'Windings of the River Forth', with its fertile valleys and amphitheatre of hills.

G7 **BRUCE AND DE BOHUN**   To the standard of Robert the Bruce, Scotland's most valorous king, the Highland clans and Scottish lowland families rallied in one great effort to free their country from the yoke of the English king. The evening before the memorable victory of Bannockburn, an English knight, Sir Henry De Bohun, rode against the Scottish king, thinking to make him an easy prey. Bruce raised himself on his steed, swung its head aside, and with one blow of his battle-axe brought the ambitious knight to the ground.

G8 **DRUM CLOG**   In 1679, near Loudon Hill, a body of Covenanters fought, and gained a victory over, Claverhouse and his troops.

G9 **A BORDER RAID**   The Scots and the English had many wars over the northern counties of England, and the Lothians of Scotland. As a result, the Border countries were always in a state of turmoil and destruction. This state existed until the Union of the Crowns in 1603.

H4 **CULLODEN**   The Jacobite army was completely routed by Cumberland and the Royal forces at Culloden Moor in 1746. Prince Charles with some of his chiefs and clansmen escaped to the hills and glens, whilst the troops were given orders to search for them and put them to the sword. In this way many met their death. The wounded and dying were massacred on the battlefield.

H5 **THE MARCH FROM GLENFINNAN**   From Glenfinnan Charles and the Highland army marched towards Edinburgh. At Perth they were received with great rejoicing. The people subscribed liberally to their funds, and many from the clans in the district joined their ranks.

H6 **STIRLING CASTLE**   For centuries, Stirling Castle was the favourite residence of Scottish kings. It was the birthplace of James II, James III, and James IV. James VI spent the first thirteen years of his life here. It is one of Scotland's most ancient and historical fortresses.

I6 **CROWNING OF THE SCOTTISH KINGS**   The MacDuffs had the honour of crowning the Scottish kings. In 838 the Coronation Stone was brought to Scone and remained there until King Edward I removed it to England in 1296.

I7   **EDINBURGH CASTLE** Edinburgh Castle was impregnable as an ancient stronghold. It is now an infantry barracks. Because of its history and associations, it forms a subject of great interest to all visitors to the capital. In the Throne Room the Regalia of Scotland is kept.

I8   **BRUCE AND THE RED COMYN** Robert the Bruce and Sir John Comyn claimed the right to the Scottish throne. They met in a church in Dumfries when, during an argument, Bruce drew his dagger and wounded Comyn. He rushed outside and told his friends, Kirkpatrick and Lindsay, what he had done. 'I'll mak' sikkar', said Kirkpatrick, who then entered the church and killed the wounded man.

J2   **A SCOTTISH DESIGN**
1. The Saint Andrew's Cross or Scottish National Ensign.
2. The Thistle or Scottish National Emblem.
3. Heather and the Scottish blue bell.

J3   **THE MONARCH OF THE GLEN** There are many deer forests in the Highlands. The deer is commonly called 'The Monarch of the Glen'.

J4   **ROYAL DEESIDE** The Highland Royal residence, Balmoral Castle, is situated close by the River Dee. The estate is extensive, covering about 25,000 acres, much of which is deer forest.

J5   **THE BATTLE OF HARLAW** The title of the Earldom of Ross was contested by Donald, Lord of the Isles, on behalf of his wife. In 1411, he marched to Harlaw with 10,000 men, against an army sent by the Regent, Albany, on behalf of his son, under the command of the Earl of Mar. The two armies withdrew, completely exhausted, so that the battle was neither lost nor won. Albany, later, forced Donald to sign a treaty surrendering all claims to the title.

J7   **A LOWLAND LANDSCAPE** The beauty of the Lowlands cannot be exaggerated. Although not so mountainous and rugged as the Highlands, the countryside possesses a charm which arrests the attention of travellers and has inspired the pens of authors and poets.

J8   **A BORDER RAID** The people of the Borders suffered much from invasion. In this case it would appear that the English had been the victors, but the position was often the reverse, when the Scots would be in possession of the plunder.

K1   **VIKINGS** The Vikings were sea pirates who, in early history, landed and plundered wherever they chose.

K6   **PRINCESS MARGARET ARRIVES FROM NORWAY** The Princess Margaret married James III of Scotland. Her father, King Christian of Norway, Sweden and Denmark, gave as her dowry the Orkney and Shetland Islands. He also cancelled the debt that had been owing since the reign of James I. This debt was the result of an agreement after the Battle of Largs (F7).

K8   **THE BATTLE OF FLODDEN** There was scarcely a home that did not mourn the loss of a father, son or relative after this battle which was a sad disaster in the history of Scotland. It was fought in 1513, and the Scottish King James IV and many of his nobles were slain.

Castles and Keeps on the Clan Map

Achnagarry	E5	Hawthornden	I7
Airlie	I5	Hermitage	J8
Ardchonnel	E6	Holyrood Palace	I7
Ardtornish	D6	Home	K7
Armadale	J8	Innerwick	K7
Armstrong	D4	Inveraray	E6
Aros	D5	Invergarry	F4
Balmoral	I4	Inverlochy	F5
Bass	J6	Iona Cathedral	C6
Blair	H5	Kennedy	F9
Borthwick	I7	Keissimull	A5
Bothwell	G7	Kilchurn	E6
Braemar	I5	Kildrummie	I4
Branxholm	J8	Kinclaven	I5
Burleigh	I6	Kinclochaline	D5
Caerlaverock	H8	Linlithgow Palace	H7
Campbell	H6	Loch-an-Eilean	H4
Cawdor	G4	Loch Leven	I6
Cessford	K8	Lochmaben	I8
Clackmannan	H6	Lochslin	G3
Closeburn	H8	Loudon	G7
Craigmillar	I7	Lumphannan	J4
Crathes	J4	Macduff	I6
Crichton	I7	Methven	H6
Crookston	G7	Montgomery	F7
Culzean	F8	Moy Hall	G4
Darnick	J7	Muckrach	H4
Dean	G7	Neidpath	I7
Direleton	J6	Ness	G4
Douglas	H8	Newark	I6
Doune	G6	Philiphaugh	I7
Drum	J4	Preston	J7
Drumlanrig	H8	Roslin	I7
Duart	D6	Rothesay	E7
Duffus	H3	Roy	F5
Dunbar	J7	Ruthven	H6
Dumbarton	F7	Seton	J7
Dundonald	F7	Skipness	E7
Dunfermline Palace	I6	Spynie Palace	I3
Dunollie	E6	St Andrews	J6
Dunottar	K5	Stirling	H6
Dunskey	E9	Tarbert	E7
Dunstaffnage	E6	Tantallon	J6
Dunvegan	C4	Thirlestane	J7
Edinburgh	I7	Threave	H9
Edzell	J5	Thurso	H1
Elcho	I6	Tillietudlem	H7
Elphinston	J7	Torthorwald	I8
Falkland Palace	I6	Toward	F7
Finlarig	G6	Tulloch	G3
Floors	K7	Turnberry	F8
Fyvie	J4	Urquhart	G4
Glamis	I5	Whittinghame	J7
Gylen	E6	Wick	I2
Hailes	J7	Yester	J7

Battles on the Clan Map

		Key
Aberdeen	13 September 1644	K4
Alford	2 July 1645	J4
Ancrum Moor	27 February 1545	J8
Annan	25 December 1332	I9
Auldearn	9 May 1645	H3
Bannockburn	24 June 1314	H6
Bothwell Bridge	22 June 1679	G7
Bridge of Dee	19 June 1639	J4
Carbisdale	27 April 1650	F2
Cromdale	1 May 1690	H4
Culloden	16 April 1746	G4
Dalnaspidal	26 July 1654	G5
Drumclog	1 June 1679	G7
Dunbar	3 September 1650	J7
Dundee	4 April 1645	J6
Dunkeld	21 August 1689	H5
Dunnichen	20 May 1685	J5
Dunsinane	27 July 1054	I6
Dupplin Moor	12 August 1332	I6
Falkirk I	22 July 1298	H7
Falkirk II	17 January 1746	H7
Flodden	9 September 1513	K8
Fyvie	28 October 1644	J4
Glenlivet	3 October 1594	I4
Glenshiel	10 June 1719	E4
Halidon Hill	19 July 1333	K7
Harlaw	24 July 1411	K4
Inverlochy	2 February 1645	F5
Killicrankie	27 July 1689	H5
Kilsyth	15 August 1645	G7
Langside	13 May 1568	G7
Largs	2 October 1263	F7
Lochmaben	22 July 1484	I8
Lumphanan	15 August 1057	J4
Meldrum	22 May 1308	J4
Methven	19 June 1306	H6
Otterburn	19 August 1388	K8
Philiphaugh	13 September 1645	I7
Pinkie	10 September 1547	I7
Prestonpans	21 September 1745	J7
Renfrew	20 October 1164	G7
Sark	23 October 1448	I9
Sauchieburn	11 June 1488	H6
Sheriffmuir	13 November 1715	H6
Solway Moss	24 November 1542	I8
Stirling Bridge	11 September 1297	G6
Tippermuir	1 September 1644	H6

List of Scottish Sovereigns

Malcolm II	1005-1034	First Interregnum	1290-1292
Duncan I	1034-1040	John Baliol	1292-1296
Macbeth	1040-1057	Second Interregnum	1296-1306
Malcolm III (Canmore)	1057-1093	Robert I	1306-1329
Donald Bane	1093-1094	David II	1329-1371
Duncan II	1094-1094	Robert II	1371-1390
Donald Bane (2nd Reign)	1094-1097	Robert III	1390-1406
Edgar	1097-1107	James I	1406-1437
Alexander I	1107-1124	James II	1437-1460
David I	1124-1153	James III	1460-1488
Malcolm IV	1153-1165	James IV	1488-1513
William (The Lion)	1165-1214	James V	1513-1542
Alexander II	1214-1249	Mary	1542-1567
Alexander III	1249-1286	James VI	1567-1625
Margaret (Maid of Norway)	1286-1290		

Some Sources of Further Information

Organisations
The Council of Scottish Clan Associations, P.O. Box 27268, Houston, Texas 77227
The Scottish International Gathering Trust, 25 Dublin Street, Edinburgh EH1 3PB (031-557 4059)
The Scottish Tartans Society, Davidson House, Drummond Street, Comrie, Perthshire
The Scots Ancestry Research Society, 3 Albany Street, Edinburgh EH1 3PY (031-556 4220)

Books
Adam, Frank *The Clans, Septs and Regiments of the Scottish Highlands* Edinburgh 1970
Black, George F. *The Surnames of Scotland: Their Origin, Meaning and History* New York 1946
Dorward, David *Scottish Surnames* Edinburgh 1985; *Scotland's Place Names* Edinburgh 1983
Hanks, Patrick and Hodges, Flavia *A Dictionary of Surnames* Oxford 1988
Old Scots Surnames Dalkeith 1982
World Directory of Scottish Societies Edinburgh 1980